PRAISE FOR *PLAY THE PART*

"Gina is a maestro of public speaking! She coached me for my TED talk, and I am forever grateful to her for giving me the technical and emotional training I needed to take the stage."

—Susan Cain, bestselling author of *Quiet*

"In my field of design and innovation, it's the human connections that build momentum for great ideas. Gina Barnett teaches us how to bring our full selves into every conversation, from connecting with our friends and colleagues to telling one's most personal story at TED."

—David Kelly, founder and chair of IDEO
and the Donald W. Whittier Professor in
Mechanical Engineering at Stanford University

"Gina is an incredible coach who'll increase your impact when presenting in an executive setting—or any professional interaction. But she can't be everywhere, so this book is the next best thing! A must-read."

—Greg Behar, CEO of Nestlé Health Science

"*Play the Part* is an essential guide for anyone who is interested in elevating their communication style to achieve maximum effectiveness. It teaches how crucial every part of your body is to your communication effectiveness, and all the ways that your intended message can unconsciously be hampered. *Play the Part* armed me with career-propelling tools that helped me become more self-aware and, more important, bodily aware. I now feel that I am not only heard but seen as authentically and powerfully as I hope to be."

—Lucinda Martinez, SVP of Multicultural Marketing at HBO

"Gina is the best in the business when it comes to training leaders in 'omnipresent communication,' and I'm a master of my newly discovered messaging channel, my body, because of her. *Play the Part* is a jewel for those of us who dare call ourselves great communicators."

—James Andrews, founder of True Story Agency

"Bringing her considerable warmth, sense of humor, and passion to the task, Gina teaches us how to unlock our innate ability to connect with other people. *Play the Part* is a must-read not just for business but for all communication success."

—Alexander Saint-Amand, CEO of GLG (Gerson Lehrman Group)

"Gina has a supreme knack for distilling the key essence and getting to the heart of the matter!"

—Kareem Yusuf, SVP of Development of Smarter Commerce at IBM

"Gina Barnett is a master teacher of the art of connection. Every page of this book offers valuable lessons gleaned from her rich experience with every kind of senior leader. There are lessons here for us all."

—Richard Socarides, former White House
senior advisor to President Bill Clinton

"Gina taught me how to connect to the power of my truth and convey it through storytelling. When I step onstage to share my message, the intimacy and courage I feel is all because of Gina—her generosity, her knowledge. *Play the Part* is an invaluable gift for anyone with a message to convey."

—Geena Rocero, LGBT activist and model

PLAY THE PART

PLAY THE PART

MASTER BODY SIGNALS TO CONNECT
AND COMMUNICATE FOR BUSINESS SUCCESS

GINA BARNETT

New York   Chicago   San Francisco   Athens   London   Madrid
Mexico City   Milan   New Delhi   Singapore   Sydney   Toronto

1 2 3 4 5 6 7 8 9 0   QFR/QFR   1 2 1 0 9 8 7 6 5

ISBN   978-0-07-183548-0
MHID   0-07-183548-2

e-ISBN 978-0-07-183549-7
e-MHID 0-07-183549-0

McGraw-Hill Education books are available at special quantity discounts to use as premiums and sales promotions or for use in corporate training programs. To contact a representative, please visit the Contact Us pages at www.mhprofessional.com.

*To my family: Mark Gordon, my husband, best friend,
champion, and soul mate; and our son, Max Gordon,
light of my life, delight of my heart.*

*To my parents, Norman and Flory Barnett,
for their unflagging love and support, and to my brother,
Larry, my first playmate who taught me not to fear
but to relish a great thunderstorm.*

Contents

PART I

THE STORIES OUR BODIES TELL

PART II

PRESENCE IS A SKILL NOT A GIFT

Acknowledgments

I have a problem with the myth of rugged individualism promoted in American lore. The truth is, each one of us becomes who we are as a result of the generosity of time, knowledge, love, and care given by those who came before. Not one of us learned to walk, talk, read, or think without such devotion. That said, and in the spirit of deepest gratitude, I owe all I know first to my family and then to the amazing theater artists and teachers who were my direct or indirect teachers: My thanks go to Gloria Landes, who ran a theater school for kids, where I spent nearly every Saturday of my life from the age of nine until I left for college. I thank Paul Mann, Curt Dempster, Ted Kazanoff, Charles Marowitz, John Braswell, Byrne Piven, Gates McFadden, Janet Zand (formerly Rifkin). Each was a master teacher. I was so fortunate to have had the opportunity to be trained by such dedicated and gifted artists. While I never knew her personally, I owe an enormous debt of gratitude to the great Viola Spolin, who created Games for the Theater, and Jersey Grotowski. Both invented exercises and theatrical practices that my teachers passed on to me and that I then improvised upon when I became a teacher. Many of the exercises included here are my variations on their inspiring ideas. I'll always be thankful to my amazing acting students who let me play, experiment, and create.

This book would never have happened without a major kick in my rear from Ainissa Ramirez, fellow writer, and Laura Wood, my agent. Or without Casey Ebro, my patient and very wise editor, who walked me through this, my first book. A million thanks to the amazing Chip Kidd for his inspired and playful cover design.

As with any maiden voyage, it's crucial to assemble a great team of guides. I'm forever grateful to my oldest friend, Janet Chan, for her tremendously helpful comments and suggestions. She's been a lifelong champion of all my various pursuits, and I'm lucky to have such a smart and loving friend. Many thanks as well to those early readers who guided, prodded, and pushed me to find my voice and tell it straight: Saj Nicole Joni, Kate McLoed, James Occhino, and my brother, Larry Barnett.

Finally, I am eternally grateful to my clients. You have all taught me so much. Because of you, I've had opportunities to explore cultures and styles of communication vastly different from my own, to travel the world, and to study deeply the mystery of connection. Mostly though, you've given me the profound gift of your trust. For that, I cannot thank you enough.

Dear Reader,

This is a book about the body—how it moves, relates, and impacts oneself and others. Over a hundred exercises are suggested throughout the book, many of which are physical. Should you attempt any of them—and I sincerely hope that you do, as you'll learn and experience yourself and your body in new and wonderful ways—please do so with great respect for your own physical condition and limitations. The vast majority of these exercises are gentle and not strenuous, but everyone is different. If something is too taxing or begins to feel uncomfortable, use your best judgment and stop!

INTRODUCTION
Why Play the Part?

"Only connect!"

—E. M. FORESTER

received a call one day from an HR manager at a global financial services organization. The manager wanted to discuss a high potential whom I'll call Clair. Despite Clair's remarkable intelligence and deep subject knowledge, she was unable to advance in her career; there was something in the way she presented herself that kept sabotaging all her efforts to be seen as a leader. Could I possibly help?

I met Clair in my office about three weeks later. At our first meeting I scribbled down words that popped instantly to mind: "kind, genuine, super smart, apologetic, neck, soft, scared, throat." Where did those words come from? Why did I make such rapid word choices? Based on what? How quickly do we make assessments, and do they have value? Can they be revised? What assessments are being made about us and by whom? How much control do we have over the instantaneous decisions being made about us?

Everyone's body is unique. Each has its own shape, motor skills, assets, limitations, perceptual skills, history, and memory. Every body tells a story. Also, it is through the body that life is experienced, integrated, understood, and conceptualized. Over the past two decades there has been significant inquiry into the field of embodiment, the notion that the body and how it experiences and interacts with the world is deeply integral to thought and cognition. The cognitivist point of view—which held that thought was a product of mental abstraction, symbols, and language—was the dominant perspective well before Descartes declared, "I think therefore I am." The more recent shift toward embodiment as a *source* of thought opens entirely new ways of understanding how we affect one another, how our bodies give rise to ideas, and how movement itself can be the seed of new thoughts. "I think therefore I am" might well be revised to "I walk therefore I think!"

The awareness that aspects of mind may arise *from* the body has tremendous ramifications for all aspects of communication. For what is a body but a constantly sensing instrument pulling data from other bodies and the surrounding environment? As the pendulum swings from a cognitive to an embodiment perspective, there is bound to be a middle ground that emerges. How do our bodies influence our thinking? What are the physical blocks that prevent our own self-understanding? How do those blocks prevent us from connecting with others?

The chief culprit that most often prevents connection is tension. Tension can be physical, vocal, emotional, psychological, or spiritual. No matter its source, tension creates a wall within the self and between that self and others. Quite simply, tension blocks the flow of exchange. It limits creative impulses, prevents risk taking, and literally seizes parts of the body. It can cause you to second-guess yourself, impede clear thought, and strike you dumb.

Where does tension come from? Why it is such a potent force? How is it manifest? Most importantly, what can be done to release it, control it—even exploit it? For Clair, the tension manifested in her throat. Her voice was thin, flat, and lifeless; her jaw locked tight. She ate her own sound. Why? Why was she carrying so much tension in that part of her body? Did her self-opinion shape her tension, or did her body tension impact her self-perception?

Humans evolved to send and receive countless communicative signals. A dismissive hand wave, a raised eyebrow, a habitually tucked chin, a warm smile, bewildered eyes—these all have profound, unspoken effects. Ignoring such signals vastly diminishes our ability to connect and communicate. These signals are subtextual, i.e., beneath spoken language. To navigate the innumerable bits of subtextual communication zooming by seems an impossible task, but the fact is we take in these moments. They have enormous impact on how we connect, or don't, if an exchange succeeds or fails. For the most part, this level of communication is unconscious, but it results in instantaneous decisions about how trustworthy, credible, reliable, or genuine someone is. We've survived because of these instinctive lifesaving skills. However, in our increasingly complex, competitive global marketplace—where professionals from different countries and cultures interact—it's no longer sufficient to rely solely on what's instinctive or unconscious. Success today demands a profound awareness of the signals one sends and the acute and *accurate* interpretation of those received. To survive is one thing, but to *thrive*, it is essential that we go beyond the instinctive and develop conscious mastery.

This is not a "body language" book; there are countless other titles that cover that subject. This is a "body-as-an-instrument" book. I hope to give you a deeper appreciation of how the body influences yourself and others. As a communications coach to executives, leaders, entrepreneurs, and high potentials around the world, my process is to locate and unravel the source of whatever is blocking expression, self-realization, and connection with oneself and others. Following that, my goal is to provide tools that encourage improvisation and risk *in* the present moment. Those tools are then supported by design and thinking skills that enhance and incorporate the newly learned behaviors. Fundamentally, my goal is to help my clients genuinely "live" the role each is "playing"—or "play" the role each is "living." On the surface, this may seem contradictory, but we all play numerous roles all day long: manager, mother, employee, father, customer, child; the list goes on and on. Most people shift styles organically, with little awareness of the demands of each part. But for some, the challenges are fierce.

My focus as a coach is never to make my clients "actors" or "pretenders," but rather to *remove the blocks that prevent connection*. This is a vital distinction. Removing blocks is very different from being false or faking it. Our bodies and minds house deeply ingrained habits and patterns that once discovered can be redirected or even shed to allow for new pathways, new self-images, new thoughts. Different ways to connect emerge. To identify and unravel habitual blocks that prevent connection is always my goal. Imagine a musical instrument. A tuba is not a flute is not a trombone. Each has a unique shape that results in a distinctive sound or timbre. Each has its own story or tune to play. However, if the tuba has a broken valve, or the trombone a dented slide—no matter how gifted the musician who plays that instrument—the outcome will always be influenced by the damaged part. A talented player can work around a damaged part, but the instrument will never play as richly as possible as long as the damage itself isn't addressed. It's the same with us. It is always my intention to identify where a particular client's block to connection resides and to offer ways to remedy that block and open up new channels.

The challenge is habit. We are all incredibly habit-driven, moving in the same patterns year after year, experiencing life through bodies confined by routine. Many of those routines act as filters that limit our perception and our thinking. The good news is, despite our habits, we are all "works in progress," and that's where potential lies. The body is fluid, and the brain is plastic (not "fixed") and constantly evolving. Knowing this, it's important to routinely refine and retune how we listen, move, think, and connect. Ultimately, the goal is to play the instrument in which you live robustly and joyously. As the cellist Fredrik Sjölin put it, "People who play the instrument also form the instrument." As you play the instrument that is your body, that contains your thoughts, you can remake how it experiences the world around you. Keep in mind that who you are, your personality, is well established. Personalities don't change, but *behaviors* can. Who we are is solid, but *what we do can be modified.* I'm not suggesting for a minute that making changes is easy. Old habits die hard, as the saying goes. As one CEO of a Fortune 500 company said to me, "The hardest thing for me is to remember to remember." True enough. But it is truly astonishing what can manifest when drive, focus, and will are aligned with aspirations.

Whether you are the sole proprietor or the head of a team within a corporation, the skills needed to influence, inspire, motivate, and persuade are all dependent on the efficacy, clarity, and power of your expression. Exceptional ideas cannot move people if they are not well communicated. I've seen many terrific ideas die on the vine precisely because they were poorly communicated. And we've all seen rather insubstantial ones get traction because they were so well packaged! Nonetheless, *all* communication originates and must move through and be expressed via the instrument of the body.

Increasingly, no matter the profession or business, professionals of all sorts are expected to present their ideas before varied audiences: internal stakeholders, teams, boards, clients. These audiences can be small or global. My goal is to help speakers manage a new and recent dual challenge: how to be truly present and in the moment with a live audience while at the same time appreciating that random comments, or even a well-rehearsed speech, may wind up online and quickly go global. With the ubiquity of the web and video, even seemingly private communications can be sent throughout the world in mere minutes. Presentational derailers that can prevent the clarity of connection are vast: tension that blocks the voice, unconscious habits that result in distracting hand gestures, eyes that shift around a room but never really see, to name just a few. In our wired world these need to be identified and addressed *before* any damage is done.

From years of coaching many professionals, I've come to the realization that contrary to the well-worn phrase "practice makes perfect," what practice really does is make imperfection livable. Being able to roll with the unexpected, breathe through it, accept mess-ups versus trying to hide them, be in the moment, these are the skills that practice, and *only* practice, can instill. And yet! Clients constantly tell me that they simply do not have time to practice. Make the time. Make. The. Time. There's commuting time, and lacking that, there's the shower. (Remember bathrooms have great acoustics!) A solid 10 minutes bathing and drying off are perfect for out-loud run-throughs of important upcoming messages. Speaking out loud is essential because only by saying and hearing how your words work together can you identify the places that need to be reworked, are repetitive or unclear. When we know our content inside out, feel completely comfortable with the architecture of our design, have not necessarily memorized it word for word but have a strong hold on structure, key points, and point of view, we can, as they say in the theater, throw the script in the air and truly be present.

My approach with each client is completely idiosyncratic, as no two people experience communication, managing, stage fright, or even stage panic, the same way. Nervous excitement is normal, to be expected, and can energize a talk. No matter what the platform is, whether the TED Stage or boardroom, hardly anyone speaks without some degree of stress. But audiences are generous, eager to hear new ideas or solutions to challenges. Audiences want speakers to succeed. Yet, even knowing that, the most accomplished speakers can still struggle with fears about forgetting text, losing the thread of their talk, or messing up one way or another. Since no audience can bear to watch a speaker fail, it is crucial that with all my clients, no matter what the forum, I find a way to help each to connect with ease and joy, to be centered and calm and as conversational as possible.

Whether in the boardroom or on Broadway, context is everything. (Even the most seasoned professional actor can be thrown off by knowing that someone special is in the audience.) There will always be high-stakes situations during which our bodies and emotions are hijacked by the stress response. But living in that state day in and day out—unless you *love* it—serves little purpose other than shortening your life span! Given the reality that many of us are under unremitting stress at work, must communicate constantly and present quite frequently, building the skill set to mitigate these challenges is essential. Calm authenticity is not secondary but primary. It will affect you as much as it will impact your audience.

● ● ● ● ●

I spent most of my professional life in the theater. Like many aspiring actors, I caught the bug early. I began studying at the age of nine and continued through and beyond college. I took years of classes in voice, speech, singing, modern dance, ballet, Alexander Technique, improvisation, character work, audition technique, scene study, and directing. Acting and the teaching of acting, which I did for 30 years, are a "practice" in that they cannot be learned from books, only from experience. Great acting teachers spend their lives observing human beings and behaviors to impart to their students the tools to truthfully portray them. The techniques actors use to usher audiences into imaginary worlds evolved for a primary purpose: to emotionally move those audiences. The secondary aim, to make them think, is the result of those stirred emotions. (As much as we may like to believe that we are rational creatures, emotional engagement is often the driving force behind our decisions.)

How do actors do what they do? How do they connect with each other onstage and with an audience? What are the techniques and tools they use? And can such skills be employed by all professionals not to "act" but to increase their ability to connect, inspire, motivate, and lead? My lifelong devotion to the craft of acting is what inspired me to bring those skills to those not conversant in the language of theater technique and stagecraft. I first made the transition by working with medical students. I would "act" the patient and observe how the student performed an intake interview or delivered difficult news. Then I would provide feedback. Eventually I began to work with global corporations, nonprofits, midsized companies, and arts institutions. These opportunities allowed me to work all over the world, interacting with professionals from vastly different cultures—bankers from Yemen, technical operations managers from Bangladesh, drug developers from Thailand, and finance managers from Russia, to name just a few! For many, the results have been life changing. I thought, why not write a book for nonactors that introduces them to the profoundly amazing techniques that actors master in order to connect?

In Part I, I discuss the body according to separate "centers." The head is followed by the chest and heart, the belly, the hips, the legs, and the feet. By tackling each of these body centers, my goal is to help you experience how deeply interconnected they are. Very few people realize the impact the feet have on the upper body and overall posture. The architecture of the body, when well aligned and supported by correct muscle engagement, effortlessly expresses intention. But most of us, due to either injury, habits, stress, or trauma, have interrupted or distressed that elegant structure and flow of energy. As a result, we unconsciously send mixed or unclear signals. For example, what I call a "collapsed middle"—the lower back is curved outward and the abdomen is crunched in on itself—can make a person *appear* tired or bored, while that may not be the case at all. Additionally, the effects of such a "stuck" body position, or interruption of the flow of energy, can impact a person's voice, mood, movement, receptivity, and even thoughts. Each chapter on the body's centers focuses on both the physical aspects that can impinge upon or improve connection and the metaphoric and emotional impact of a given center.

Part II addresses "Presence." Many think of presence as charisma, an innate gift, something you're either born with or not. But having spent decades training actors how to achieve presence, I know that it is both a skill and the outcome of a series of actions. Those actions, available to all of us, involve listening keenly, being fully engaged with what's happening "right now," trusting not only your knowledge and expertise but also your gut. Presence, or full engagement in *this* moment combined with a preawareness of situational demands and expectations, is not innate. All these actions are performed by the body in concert with the mind. They are skills, not mysteries.

To be most effective, one's "presence" needs to be aligned with clear communication. The skills needed to design clear and effective communication are introduced via key messaging. This is an organization tool with wide application. Beyond the needs of presenting ideas, key messaging is terrific for problem solving, negotiations, strategy design, managing, and even self-exploration. It is a tool that, if used routinely, becomes second nature. The result? Increased presence. Why? Because the alignment of body awareness with well-designed thinking processes improves communication efficiency. Clarity and efficiency impact how we are perceived. How we are perceived in turn influences our presence, because presence is not a one-way street. It's a combination of our thoughts and behaviors and our audiences' reactions to those behaviors in a constant flow back and forth. Moment-by-moment presence is a dynamic in constant flux.

What happens when, increasingly, we are not communicating in the same space but only virtually? What is the impact of presence and communication when it is increasingly mediated by technology? While there is no doubt that the ability to hold meetings in real time with large numbers of people who are physically scattered across the globe has great benefit, the risks of such interactions must be appreciated as well. Relationships, listening, and understanding can all be unexpectedly and instantaneously derailed. Social media, texts, e-mails, avatar meetings, all these will no doubt look quite primitive one day. For now, their implications are great. While it seems an extreme schism might exist between those who grew up pre-Internet and those born well after its development, given the rapid and ever-evolving nature of these technologies, such difficulties will most likely be a constant. I examine how to keep creating new and better ways to connect in light of increasing and rapid technological changes.

In his book *The Code of the Executive*, Don Schmincke takes 47 ancient samurai principles and applies them to leadership success in the twenty-first century. In his introduction, he asks the reader who may choose to skip around the text to, if nothing else, read the first and most controversial chapter. If the reader feels resistance to some of the ideas, he suggests giving oneself "permission to suspend avoidance of discomfort." (What a great combination of words! In the theater it's called "the willing suspension of disbelief.") Mr. Schmincke is asking the reader to take in the words no matter what they evoke. And how does that first and most important chapter open?

"One who is an executive must before all things keep constantly in mind, by day and by night, the fact that he has to die."

What an opening! Deep down we all know this to be true, but hardly any of us do the daily reminder that forces us to believe it. It is precisely the reminder of our mortality that opens the portal to presence in this very moment. Presence— the courage to be fully alive in every moment in time, to take risks, to align one's work with one's values, to imagine, and to play—is available to all but accessed by few.

To that end, throughout the book, I suggest exercises to explore and experience under the heading "Try This." The tools and tips are not "instructions"; rather, they are practices and experiences that can help to identify and modify habits that prevent connecting with the present moment. Whether you are a leader, team player, or sole entrepreneur, the tools are designed to increase communication efficacies, identify where your body instrument might need repair, and offer fun and challenging ways to do so. It's my hope that by giving them a try, you'll play your part in this awesome singular life you now, but so briefly, possess. Be forewarned: many of the exercises will be challenging and quite foreign to your experience. I ask only that you give yourself "permission to suspend avoidance of discomfort." There is an appendix (Appendix B) where you can easily find the exercises that will be most beneficial to you. For example, vocal challenges and exercises are in various chapters throughout the book. But in Appendix B, they are all found in one section under "Vocal Mastery—Volume, Resonance, Tone, Enunciation." Treat this text as you would a workbook. Should you commit to any long-term efforts, you can keep track of your progress using worksheets provided at the end of each chapter and at the end of the book. You may use the worksheets to keep track of:

- The exercises you choose to do
- How often you intend to do them
- How often you actually do them
- The results you observe
- Any self-generated next steps you plan to take

The goal is to enable you not only to monitor your progress but to note any subtle changes that result. (For instance, a client recently told me that an exercise I gave her to slow down her rate of speaking had improved how she expressed herself, as well as her overall executive presence.) I encourage you to make up your own variations on both the exercises and the worksheet templates.

The biggest challenge for all of us is time. People think that to incorporate new behaviors and break old habits requires not only the resolve to change but lots of time. But the good news is that you already have the time; you just don't know it. We all have daily rituals that we do with little or no thought. I remember when my mother quit smoking, she joined an organization called Smoke Enders. The first thing Smoke Enders instructed her to do was write down her smoking rituals and then find alternatives. So, for example, if she always carried her lighter tucked in her pack of cigarettes, she should keep the lighter in the freezer or somewhere totally inconvenient. This delay would give her time to ask herself, "Do I really need this cigarette right now?" The goal was to interrupt ritual and replace it with intention. That is my recommendation to you as well.

Observe one of your daily rituals: waking up, making coffee, getting dressed, starting your car. Once you've broken down the steps, take a moment to insert one of the tips you wish to practice right in the middle of an already established ritual. Many of the tips suggested take a very short amount of time to do—but they must become routine to result in the desired changes.

● ● ● ● ●

Returning to Clair, what was it about her style and voice that made me jot down "scared"? She had come to see me at my office a couple of times, but for our third meeting, I went to hers. I entered and was immediately struck by the sweeping views she had of Manhattan, south toward Radio City and the Empire State Building, west toward the glorious Hudson River.

"Wowie," I gushed with awe and delight. "This city, it still takes my breath away. And seeing this view out your window every day, that's so amazing. How fabulous for you."

"I don't deserve it," she mumbled. I was dumbstruck, mystified. I looked at her and I waited. "I'm from this little tiny town in Wyoming. I'm a small-town girl. What am I doing here? This shouldn't be mine."

"But you've earned it. It *is* yours. You did earn it, did you not?"

A reluctant nod was all I got back. How could she speak up with energy, intelligence, and confidence if deep down she doubted her right to her very own well-earned position?

I turned to Clair and, with an imaginary royal sword, I solemnly declared, "I dub you queen." She laughed. "Seriously. You are queen, and this—all of this— is yours. You've earned it. Look around you. You own it: this room, this view, that river, every building. It *all* belongs to you." She had no idea what to do. "Play with me," I winked. "Be the queen. What's the harm? Let's explore how it will feel for you to actually give yourself permission to own what you have earned."

She said nothing. Carefully, but with total conviction, I added an imaginary jewel-encrusted crown, red velvet cape, and gold staff. "Your Highness," I whispered and bowed. Clair grew three inches before my eyes. "I beseech you to make fruitful all these lands within your domain."

A voice deep and sonorous emerged from her body. "I shall grant your wish."

"Your Highness, might you walk with me and show me all that you possess?"

And with that, Clair took me on a royal constitutional around her office, elaborating on all her accomplishments and acquisitions.

"And those buildings below?"

"Mine! All mine!" she bellowed.

"Done!" I said, snapping my fingers and ending the magic. I looked at her. "Clair, up until now, you've been a small-town girl. But from this moment on, you are a queen."

"My goodness," Clair was beaming. "How did that happen? How did you do that?"

"Play?" I responded. "We all can play, if we just give ourselves permission." (I'm still amazed by how quickly my clients, no matter how senior, will jump into an imaginary on-the-spot improvisation with me. As if by magic anyone—CEO or SVP—can be five again!)

Clair replied, "But I can't walk around like that all the time. It's not me. It's too showy and grand and not truly who I am."

"Being a small-town girl isn't truly who you are either. Not anymore. Your truth is an outdated construct of who you've become, and it's keeping you stuck. I'm not asking you to walk around all the time as the royal 'we.' I'm suggesting you give yourself permission to own what you have earned. Only then will you be able to confidently share your knowledge, skills, experience."

"But!"

"No buts, Your Highness! Now, let us again take another royal walk." And we did. Or rather she walked, and I followed obsequiously behind.

"This feels amazing," she sang. But resistance is fierce. "But, still . . . *it's not me.*"

"Really?" I asked. "How do you know? Who says?"

Who are any of us? We are often so much more than we allow ourselves to be. We imagine, we dream, we fantasize, and then we slip back into our concept of reality, rarely questioning if that concept has *any relation to the truth*. Furthermore, that concept, like Clair's, lives in the body, becomes ingrained as muscle memory and habitual, limited patterns of movement. Despite her success, Clair's self-conceptualization was stuck in a true but antiquated idea of herself. The body she presented, with its small voice and tight throat, was that of her self-conception as a small-town girl. Playing queen, even for a few short moments, allowed her to feel different, see things with a new perspective, and break the bonds of outdated physical and mental constructs.

Play the Part is a business book on communication. But the title's first word is "*Play*," and it is so for an important reason. Play is seriously missing from our lives. Why do children play? Because by playing teacher, or mommy, or astronaut, children let curiosity open the portal to their imagined selves. They try on an "other" to find themselves. As our world becomes increasingly stressed on so many levels, each of us must seek ways to bring back play. While the drive to make babies is clearly first and foremost to propagate the species, it has been my long-term suspicion that the second reason is to give our serious adult selves permission to freely indulge in joyous play. Why? Because play is powerful. Rooted in imagination and curiosity, it is available to each and every one of us. We don't need to ask anyone but our own rigid selves for permission to play. Once embraced, its impact is stunning.

Within the next 18 months Clair, who'd been stuck in the same role for years, got two promotions. Did her evolution happen overnight? Absolutely not. It required profound shifts in self-conception, point of view, carriage, and imagination. Play is serious.

In that spirit, I ask only that you think of *Play the Part* not as an instruction manual but as a conversation with yourself. Think of this book not as a "how-to" but a "why-not?" Oh, and have fun!

PART I

THE STORIES OUR BODIES TELL

Use Your Head

*"You can go a long way with
bad legs and a good head."*
— GAVIN MCDONALD

'll never forget my second grade teacher, Miss Murphy, quizzing our class on how to greet a stranger. "What is the first thing you should do after you open the door?" she asked. Hands shot up.

"Yes, Billie?"

"Shake hands."

"Good answer, but that's not the *first* thing. Susan?"

"Say hello?"

"Another good answer, but that's not the very *first* thing."

Others offered ideas. All were sensible but not the answer she was looking for. Seven years old and we were stumped. Finally, Miss Murphy saved us from our befuddlement. "Smile," she said.

I think about that second grade lesson quite often these days as I pose a variation of her question to my clients. Surprisingly, what I encounter isn't wrong answers, but resistance to the correct one. It's made me wonder just what it is about *smiling* that makes people so profoundly uncomfortable? Men think it weak or phony to smile; women worry it undermines the little power they've attained. I had one client go so far as to say, "I'll have to work on perfecting a fake smile that *looks* genuine." Perfect a *fake* smile? Really? Why not just smile and mean it? Why is there such resistance to joy, pleasure, or just sheer warmth?

No matter how many reasons people come up with for not smiling, I suspect the deepest reasons relate to the vulnerability of the mouth itself. When we part our lips, we reveal—and revealing is *risky*. Clients have told me over the years that to show emotion, or overtly feel, is perceived as weakness. To be open is to leave oneself open. Juniors in the workplace observe serious-minded seniors and determine that to succeed, one must look grim. Those in middle management tell themselves that smiling diminishes credibility and authority. No matter why people feel compelled to repress their warmth, the results are pretty universal: clenched jaws, mumbled words, dour expressions.

This chapter will focus on the head—in truth, an entire book could be written about the subject, as so much happens there! I'll first explore the impact of physical attributes and choices, such as whether or not to smile. Then I'll discuss the mouth, jaw, head-neck placement, eyes, and ears. The focus will then shift to internal processes, such as listening and point of view. This approach of separating physical aspects of the body from the internal, thinking, and metaphoric aspects is a completely false division. Why? Because there is a continuous body-emotion-thought feedback loop functioning in all of us *all the time*. By trying out the suggested exercises, my hope is that you'll consciously experience this body-emotion-thought loop in action and discover the impact it has on both yourself and those around you.

● ● ● ● ●

Nancy Etcoff, a clinical instructor in psychology at Harvard Medical School and the author of *Survival of the Prettiest: The Science of Beauty*, said the image we project can influence our destiny. "Research shows there are a lot of advantages for people who are considered beautiful or attractive, everywhere from the boardroom to the bedroom. . . . The same is true for people who tend to make positive expressions. . . . *And the act of smiling, even if it is forced, can be self-fulfilling in that it can on its own elevate the mood.*" (Italics mine.) Why might this be? Simple: the impact of a smile is not just felt by the person doing it. Smiling is contagious, both on the faces and in the minds of its observers.

The smile, while a universal facial expression, has different meanings in different cultures. In the United States it signals friendliness and joy; in Korea smiling can be seen as representing shallowness. In other Asian cultures it can indicate confusion or distress. Whatever the particular cultural meaning assigned to smiling, the gesture itself is embedded in human communication. (In the United States, until Teddy Roosevelt, few presidents smiled in public settings.) While many in business consider smiling counterproductive to signaling authority, its absence creates other problems. The truth is, the body and emotions are *not* separate; they profoundly affect each other. As the psychologist William James wrote in 1892, "Thus the sovereign voluntary path to cheerfulness, if our spontaneous cheerfulness be lost, is to sit up cheerfully, to look around cheerfully, and to act and speak as if cheerfulness were already there." We all know that when we're happy, smiling comes effortlessly. What we need to learn is that the act of smiling itself can lift our and others' moods. Whether or not the resistance to smiling is cultural, not smiling, with its attendant mouth and jaw tension, can engender feelings that are the antithesis of joy. We catch each other's emotions quickly and without conscious awareness, and emotions are almost always made manifest in the face. I think my second grade teacher was on to something profound.

TRY THIS: HAPPY/SAD MOUTH

Put your lips in the position your mouth goes to when you feel sad. What happens? What do you feel internally just by moving your lips? Now tighten the lips and clench the jaw as you might when angry. What happens? Now smile just a little bit. What do you feel? Now smile broadly. Try a fake smile. Now think of someone you adore or a happy memory and let the mouth organically go where it feels right. Notice how quickly the mere thought affects the mouth position and how a mouth position triggers a subtle change of emotion. It's my supreme pleasure to introduce you to the body-emotion two-way street! Welcome! We are just getting started.

What happens in those first moments when strangers meet? The handshake, facial expressivity, eye contact, vocal tone, head-neck alignment, and a multitude of other factors are instantaneously processed by the brain. As we size others up—is this stranger smart, trustworthy, confident, arrogant, warm?—they are doing the same with us. The signals sent are complex, instant, and powerful. As the saying goes, "You don't have a second chance to make a first impression."

Functional MRI technology now allows us to peer into the brain as processes occur. With the ability to probe into previously hidden aspects of brain function and activity, our understanding of smiling is deepening and is especially interesting when understood in light of mirror neurons. Currently, these neurons are understood to be a widely dispersed class of brain cells described by researchers as a kind of neural Wi-Fi. They were serendipitously discovered in the 1990s and are a special class of cells that fire when an individual merely observes someone performing an action, even though the observer isn't *doing* that action. The implications of this are yet to be fully understood. We know that the rapid synchronization of people's paces, gestures, and postures as they interact has long been observed. The result is a feeling of rapport and alignment. Then there is the concept of emotional contagion, in which one person literally catches the strongly expressed feelings and emotions of another. Imagine yourself coming into work feeling OK but running into the chronic complainer. You chat briefly, and as you walk away, you find yourself feeling irritated and no longer OK. Sound familiar? That's emotional contagion. This too may soon come to be understood in light of this neural brain-to-brain Wi-Fi of mirror neurons.

This merging of separate bodies into a connected circuit has been defined by the psychologists Lisa M. Diamond and Lisa G. Aspinwall as "a mutually regulating *psychobiological* unit." (Just think of how contagious yawning is. I've even caught the "yawns" from my dog!) We're beginning to understand how the *biology* of one person can affect and *even change* the biology of another. If merely *observing* an action activates the same brain areas as that of the person performing the action, then this extremely rapid brain-to-brain mirroring will cause *physiological* effects in *both* people. Think of a stressful business meeting and recall how quickly strongly expressed emotions provoke equally strong emotions in others. Almost instantly, all around the room, heart rates jump, breathing shallows, and palms sweat. One person's hostile remarks can trigger another's blood pressure to spike. How can this be? Because we are not alone in these bodies. We are social beings bound together in systems of continuously mutually regulating interactions. The social script that we write together is impacted by all our bodies as they express themselves physically, but also as our brains mentally reenact what we witness. Perhaps by enabling us to "catch" each other's emotions, mirror neurons will be revealed as the source of empathy. Whatever their cause or source, the next time you catch yourself refusing to smile because of how it may make you "appear," remember that by allowing yourself to smile, you very likely may be creating an invisible smile in the minds of your observers. Your warm smile might also calm another's anxiety. Wouldn't that be a great way to initiate a successful connection?

THE MOUTH

The mouth is an emotional center of enormous power. Many steps in the progression from infancy to toddlerhood are marked via the mouth. The mouth is where the first bond between infant and mother is created. As the months go by, babies explore objects with their mouths well before they refine the use of their hands. Infants' mouths will frequently twist into grimaces of despair well before you hear their first wails. Smiling occurs at around eight weeks of age and, irrespective of culture, is a much anticipated benchmark of development. It is also well rewarded with jubilantly returned smiles from parents. Early babbling is happily encouraged, as is drinking from a bottle and eventually eating with a spoon. Feeding oneself is a milestone of achievement. Each of these stages of growth is navigated via the mouth, and all occur before speech even enters the picture!

As adults, beyond dental care and grooming, few of us give much consideration to our mouths. But how lips move, jaws release, and tongues create sounds are all vital aspects of communication. (A number of excellent books are available on the voice, vocal production, speech, and accent reduction, which

I've listed in Appendix C, so I won't go into too much detail here regarding that aspect of the mouth and its role in speech.) I'll focus on the critical, micro-emotional messages the mouth sends, as these are powerful indicators of a person's inner emotional life.

What I encounter most frequently in the business world, where clear communication is essential, is minor lockjaw. People—whether it is because they are in a rush to express their thoughts, hide the feeling behind their words, or unconsciously wish *not* to be heard—open their mouths the smallest possible amount in order to speak. The result: rushed, mumbling speech is difficult to engage with or even understand. Jaw tension may be the result of something physical, but often it's rooted in something emotional. The most extreme example of self-muzzling I encountered was with a client in global banking. She was a brilliant analyst with a specialty in regulatory affairs, but she was almost impossible to hear because she literally ate her own voice. Her jaw hardly opened when she spoke; she projected her sound backward into her throat rather than out into the air. Her volume was low and her enunciation fuzzy from lack of movement. I put my hands on the muscles beside the jaw hinge and urged her to relax and let her mouth hang open. The tears were instantaneous. As a child she'd been molested by a neighbor who told her he'd kill her if she ever spoke of it. She never had. Instead she cut off her own voice. This deep trauma lived on in the story her body was telling. Granted, this was a very extreme case. Nonetheless, when growing up, who of us was never told to shut up? Many were told that repeatedly. How each body managed that instruction is unique. For some, it was of absolutely no consequence; for others, it resulted in lifelong self-silencing.

Much of our physical life is on automatic pilot. Systems and habits are laid down early in our development. Most of us pay little to no attention to our bodies as we move through our workday. Granted, pain will slow us down or stop us, awaken us to our physical self. Otherwise, we rarely take the time to tune in to the richness that is contained in our physical being. We should. Our bodies house our histories, our reactions to events and our current and past emotions. Many physical responses are conditioned by factors about which we have limited or no conscious recall. (We'll explore that more deeply in Chapter 3 on the gut.)

The mouth vividly manifests our feelings: joy, rage, disgust, sadness, fear. We can't read each other's thoughts, but we can become far more attuned to others' feelings by observing faces in general and mouths in particular. Recall for a moment how quickly your feelings changed by making subtle lip and mouth movements in the exercise "Happy/Sad Mouth." The irony about frozen or locked jaws, if one looks beneath the surface to the subtextual signals being sent, is that they can reveal as much as they seek to conceal.

TRY THIS: SWEET APRICOT: JAW RELAX

Observe if your upper and lower teeth are touching or pressing together when your mouth is shut. If so, a good way to approach relaxing the jaw is to imagine you have half a fresh apricot resting on the tongue. This will help you drop the tongue and release the pressure between the teeth, which should not be pressed together. This position, coupled with imagining the apricot, will gently relax the muscles that tend to clench the jaw.

Why do this? To consciously attune yourself to those muscles and to notice if you have chronic jaw tension. Do you grind your teeth? If you do, ask yourself, is this preventing my ability to enunciate, to be heard and understood? After relaxing your mouth, gently rub the muscles at the jawline in a circular motion to deepen the relaxation.

HEAD-NECK ALIGNMENT

Jaw tension is not a singular event and is often the result of how the head sits on the neck. With many of us now spending almost all day at our computers, often after long commutes by car or train, there's an epidemic of what I call "head thrust." The upper back is curved in on itself, and the head lurches so far forward that it's several inches in front of the chest and sticks out like that of a turtle. Proper placement of the head upon the neck has great impact not only on the voice but on how one appears and is thus *perceived*, and even more critically on *how one feels.*

The head weighs approximately 10 pounds, not all that much. Imagine holding a 10-pound weight in your hand with that hand held straight up in the air. By holding the hand perfectly upright in that position, the wrist, elbow, and shoulder all the way down to the hips and feet will enable you to support the weight. Now imagine moving that 10-pound weight forward by just a few inches. The effort required to hold those 10 pounds will be dramatically different; the muscles will have to work much, much harder to hold the weight in place. It's the same with the head. A head that juts far forward of where it is structurally designed to sit demands extensive and exhausting muscle work to hold it there. Over time those muscles wind up shifting the inner skeletal structure itself.

One of the first places our eyes go for information about someone is that person's head-neck alignment. We can see immediately if a head is "held high," tucked in on itself, or weakly supported with poor posture. On the most superficial level, a head that sits properly on the neck—is flexible, supported, and aligned—immediately sends messages of strength, health, and energy. How does it do this? It takes strength to support the head correctly. It takes energy to maintain good alignment and posture. Correcting improper head-neck alignment is a process that requires effort. Just telling yourself to sit up straight will not correct 10 to 20 years of incorrect alignment, although reminding oneself to do so is a good first step.

Keep in mind that the body is structurally built at the skeletal level for posture that enables maximal motion and flexibility. Awareness that proper alignment is vital for signaling presence, power, and confidence can make it easier to start making small changes. I had a client who was quite tall and had severe head thrust. His head was literally about three inches in front of his body. When I pointed it out and suggested he work to correct his head-neck alignment, he responded, "I've always been like this. It's the way I'm built." I told him my concern was that his posture made him look as if he were "asking" rather than "telling." "It's not the look of a leader," I said. Ambition won out, and after "always been," he quickly shifted to "better become," and within weeks he corrected his posture.

Another client, who was being groomed for a C-suite position, was sent to me because, despite his intelligence, he was not perceived as a leader. His head was tilted to the left, with his left shoulder raised toward his left ear. This head tilt shortened the muscles along the left side of his neck and shoulder, sending subtextual signals that could be perceived in a number of counterproductive ways. Despite his intelligence, he looked crumpled and unsure, doubtful of himself and others. His seniors were concerned that if he had to announce grave decisions while appearing so unsure, it could have negative outcomes.

Another client, EVP of a significant financial institution who was being groomed for advancement, had poor posture that resulted in his tendency to tuck in his chin. This had numerous consequences: a mumbling vocal tone, a flat vocal melody, a stern countenance from peering up from under his eyebrows. These factors combined to send a complex set of signals: the flattened tone made him seem dull and tired; the countenance made him appear irritated and impatient; the rounded shoulders made him seem unfit for greater leadership. This physical stature made him appear anything but "presidential." He responded to my suggestions for improving his head placement and posture by saying, "I've seen a lot of empty suits in my day who look the part but have nothing of substance to deliver." I replied that empty suits certainly exist, but my concern was that the persona he projected was not *commensurate with the role being played*.

I mention these three clients because as a communications coach, I never seek to impose choices that result in inauthentic or fake behaviors. My goal *is to help the client get rid of counterproductive, unconscious physical habits that obscure the full potential of his or her power and expressivity.* As people move up professionally, they often have to adjust their physical habits to more appropriately embody new roles. While people completely understand and accept this as it concerns professional attire, they rarely think about how it concerns head placement! But it is precisely because we make such instantaneous decisions about one another that counterproductive postures can have long-term implications.

Social psychologist Marshall McLuhan said, "The medium is the message." The form of delivery is as significant as the content being delivered. (Twitter anyone?) As a communicator, you *are* the medium; your body is the medium through which your content is delivered. For this reason alone, it is essential to have alignment of body *and* message.

As with smiling, proper or poor head-neck alignment will impact our and others' feelings and emotions. I've encountered similar resistance to it. Some statements were downright stunning: "Standing up straight is arrogant and pompous." To the contrary, authority, alertness, gravitas, intelligence—all are signaled by a well-aligned head-neck relationship. "It's tiring." Also untrue. Proper alignment, while not necessarily requiring less muscle recruitment, requires less effort. "It's unnatural." Bah! One of my all-time favorites: "So, all I have to do is stand up straight and people will think I'm an expert?" If only life could be so simple! Such arguments mask the deep resistance to the physical and mental work required to fight not only gravity but inertia and a lifetime of bad habits.

Change is hard. Habits are ingrained. Resistance is often the first thing I encounter when I make a suggestion. "Yes but" is a phrase I've heard countless times. When I was a child, teachers often said, "There's no such word as *can't*." As a coach, I often hear myself asking, "You can't or you won't? There's a difference." Resistance is normal. It's everywhere. (Friction is resistance!) Reflection, or taking the time to consider why we resist change, is an important first step, but things mustn't stop there. We have to actively engage with our reluctance to make change, to question if the resistance is well founded and purposeful or if it stems from laziness or, most critical, fear. In my experience, most people who really push back and resist incorporating suggestions for improvement are afraid. It's like being in a roaring river and holding onto a rock for dear life. If you hold on, you'll die; if you let go, you'll be swept away. Either choice is terrifying. But letting go just *may* allow the currents to carry you to safety. Or not. It is impossible to know. The only certainty is that holding on will keep you stuck. We cling to the known precisely because it *is* known. What change will usher in is unknowable, so we resist it. Only when familiar habits become obstacles to success do we begin to welcome change. Fear of failure supersedes fear of the unknown, and resistance begins to give way to curiosity and openness. My question is, why wait? When resistance rears its head, ask yourself, "What am I afraid of? What will happen if I let go and allow the current of change to carry me somewhere unknown?"

TRY THIS: HEAD HINGE

Let's play with head position. Imagine you are in a meeting. Tilt your head down and look up from underneath your eyebrows. Hold that position for 30 seconds. What do you feel? What do you imagine others might see? Now do the opposite. Lift the chin up by two inches and look "down your nose." Notice how the back of the neck shortens? Hold that for 30 seconds. What do you feel? These are extremes, but they give a good idea of how much subtext could be projected through such a position. Something as simple as attaining a level chin position can have a big impact.

TRY THIS: BROKEN BRIDGE

As you sit with this book in your hands, begin to slump. Let the head droop, the shoulders curl forward, and the belly collapse. Put your lips in a downward, sad expression. Sit like that for 30 seconds and notice how you begin to feel. Sad? Bored? Tired? Just plain blah? By experimenting with these positions, you can immediately experience how the physical positions impact emotions. Play with varied facial expressions to see what subtle emotions emerge.

We all know that when we feel sad, the body responds and looks sad. The above exercises are another way to consciously experience how *posture impacts emotion*. Furthermore, if you stayed in the slumped position described above for any period of time, not only you but those around you would begin to feel depleted of energy. Mirror neurons show us that contagion has physical as well as emotional ramifications.

There are multiple ways to address chronic head-neck misalignment, but what is most crucial is the willingness to do so. Unlike breathing, which we do automatically—but often incorrectly, more on that later—posture requires attention. To maintain proper alignment of the head, the core muscles of the abdomen must be employed. Good posture does not happen in the shoulders, but in the deep core muscles of the belly and back, where the innermost muscles surrounding the middle and lower spine engage. Sometimes, to correct decades of misuse, it is essential to work with a professional who understands the body, who can analyze your particular patterns and determine what muscle recruitment and strengthening exercises are necessary. That professional, be it physical therapist, Pilates instructor, or Alexander Technique teacher, can then give you daily exercises that target the necessary muscles to get the spine back to where it should be. In time, what was an enormous effort becomes second nature as the body self-corrects. Whichever route you take, what is most critical—as in all other aspects of change—is repeated practice. The good news is that brief repetition of corrective exercises, performed daily or every other day, can make a real difference rather quickly.

What is fascinating about the mind-body relationship is the increasing understanding of how even imagining a physical act can impact new—correct—muscle recruitment. If, for example, I suggest that you imagine an umbrella, your mind's eye will create that image. Picture a snake. Now a tulip. Visual imagery engages the part of the brain where things you have seen with your eyes have been stored as pictorial memories. But there is kinesthetic imagery stored in the brain as well. Imagine yourself swimming. Now imagine running or pouring a cup of coffee. As you imagine these movements, your brain is performing the movement.

One theory for this is that the brain must emulate movement before it is actually performed. Imagine how effortlessly we pick up a glass. The hand knows exactly how far to go. Imagine going into your pitch-black bedroom. Your hand knows precisely where the light switch is. Conversely, imagine entering an unfamiliar location and randomly patting the wall, searching for the switch! We predict, and the brain does so beforehand as a way to navigate our constantly changing and complex environment. Over the years I've observed numerous musicians on the bus or subway in New York City mentally rehearsing for a concert. Without moving a finger, they mentally "play" through a piece. Studies have shown that this form of rehearsal has profound benefits. Similarly, once you have begun to master proper head-neck placement, merely imagining the body in the correct position can have great benefit. When a physical action is mentally rehearsed, it actually *changes* the brain's motor map and the body follows along.

The take-away from the above exercises is not merely that slumping impacts appearance and shifts emotion and energy, but that good posture radiates strength, engenders energy, and actually *makes you feel better*. This is not to say that everyone needs to look the same to manifest energy and presence. I've worked with amazing individuals who are wheelchair-bound or have severe scoliosis or other postural handicaps. Despite any handicap, one can still project confidence and conviction through many other means of communication—voice, eyes, facial expression, gestures—which we will also explore. Nonetheless, whether we like to admit it or not, we all make rapid judgments about people's credibility, trustworthiness, and reliability based on very subtle cues that are instinctively assessed. It is far better to attempt mastery over head-neck alignment, posture, and the emotional and physical signals sent than not.

The first thing we instinctively do when we feel or are threatened is to pull our neck back, hunch our shoulders, and cower. The stresses of the modern day, while not akin to those of hundreds of thousands of years ago, still trigger the same autonomic responses. The amygdala, a primitive brain structure within the limbic system that's deeply involved with survival, emotions, and memory, doesn't know the difference between a leaping lion and a dirty look from a colleague. Either will set off the survival alarm, boost cortisol (the stress hormone) levels in the brain, and trigger the fight, flight, or freeze response. Recent studies by Amy Cuddy, professor and researcher at Harvard Business School, explore the connection between posture and stress response. Cuddy discovered that consciously putting the body in what she terms a "power position"—in which the body claims and occupies space with an erect posture, either arms spread wide or hands behind the head and elbows out to the sides—and holding that position for two minutes changes the chemical balance in the bloodstream. Holding a power position for as little as two minutes lowers cortisol and increases testosterone (the courage hormone), hormonal changes that can affect thinking and behavior.

Before you head into a stress-inducing conversation or presentation, try holding a power position for two minutes, take a few deep breaths, and see how you can both boost your confidence and calm yourself down.

THE VOICE

The voice exits the body through the mouth, but its source is the breath. The structure and shape of the body create resonance and timbre. I will cover the voice as it works its way through various centers of the body subsequently and in much greater depth in Chapter 2, but as far as posture is concerned, a strong head-neck relationship is essential for a relaxed, open sound. One result of head thrust is vocal fry. Jutting the head forward puts strain on the throat and on the vocal cords; the sound that emerges is hoarse, thin, dry, and crackly. Over the long term, inflamed cords or even nodes can result. At a recent presentation I attended, a speaker had severe vocal fry. About 20 seconds into her presentation, people all around the room began clearing *their* throats. Why? Her fry made them aware of their own throats, and unconsciously they were signaling for her to clear hers. Or quite possibly it was those mirror neurons again.

TRY THIS: WET DOG

Shake out your body for a few seconds, like a dog shaking water off its coat. Do a few shoulder rolls and gentle head rolls. Yawn a few times to open the throat. Take a nice deep breath and stick out the tongue and speak, with the tongue extended far out of the mouth. Do this for a minute or so. Relax and now speak normally. Do you notice a change in how the voice resonates? Is it more open and relaxed sounding?

The goal for the voice is to suit the intention of the communication. A voice should be easy to hear and understand as well as pleasant to listen to. The best way to achieve a relaxed, open, pleasant voice is to have a relaxed body. Almost all vocal challenges are the result of tension that is located somewhere along the route of vocal production. Tension, whether in the belly, chest, throat, jaw, or mouth, will impact the voice overall. But since this chapter focuses on the head, what's most critical is to be aware of how something as minor as an upturned chin or a clenched jaw can impinge on the resonance, volume, and enunciation of the voice and speech.

TRY THIS: HEAD HINGE WITH VOICE

Repeat the "Head Hinge" exercise, raising the chin a few inches, and this time recite your name, address, and phone number with your head held in that upward position. What happens in the throat? How does the voice change? Now drop the chin a few inches, lowering the head, and again recite your name, address, and phone number. What do you notice about the sound of your voice by playing with the position of the head? Now come to a level position. Yawn, stick the tongue out, and speak your name and address with your tongue out. And finally, keeping a level head with the jaw relaxed and tongue in a normal position, speak again. What do you notice?

TRY THIS: REVERSE TURTLE NECK

If from doing the above exercise you discovered that you generally keep either your position tilted or your head thrust forward, there is a very simple remedy for proper head placement. This exercise awakens, lengthens, and strengthens the often underutilized muscles at the back of the neck. *Make sure that your head is level and tilted neither up nor down.* (The best way to do this is by looking straight ahead and into a mirror. We often cannot feel a habit of head tilt up or down.) Place two fingers on your chin and very gently press the chin back toward the spine. The head might move just a half inch or so, but you'll feel the muscles in the back of your neck engage. The tendons and muscles at the front of the neck should not engage at all. Hold for 10 seconds and release. This can also be done without the fingers. While standing in an elevator or at a red light, make sure the head is level and gently bring the chin back and hold for 5 to 10 seconds. (If you do this with the head tilted slightly upward, then it will actually be counterproductive and increase the shortening of the muscles at the back of the neck. That's exactly what this exercise is designed to prevent.) If repeated throughout the day, in time, you will begin to hold your head without jutting it too far forward on the neck. Again, be extra careful to make sure that your head is level when doing this.

EYES

The eyes are powerful. Eye contact is essential. Guarded eyes, welcoming eyes, bored, tired, shifty, cruel—much is communicated via these two glassy orbs. Actually, a lot of eye signaling is accomplished by the tiny muscles surrounding the eyes that allow us to squint, smile, and frown. It's said that should the muscles around the eyes not engage when smiling, the smile will be perceived as cursory instead of heartfelt.

The eyes send and receive simultaneously. But what precisely do they send? The signals that emanate from the eyes are powerful indications of one's security, intelligence, warmth, openness, humor, strength, and leadership. Conscious control of one's eye use can best be understood by watching great film actors in close-up, and I highly recommend renting films with exceptional actors to study how they use their eyes and the muscles that surround their eyes to communicate specific messages. (Dustin Hoffman and Meryl Streep come to mind as two masters of extraordinarily subtle eye expressivity.)

Never forget that how eyes communicate is as much culturally as personally determined. I work with a number of men from the Middle East who do not make eye contact with women. It is culturally against their upbringing. I've had male clients tell me that locking eyes, a technique used in active listening for effective Q&A, is impossible because they'll be perceived as sexual or flirtatious. Clients from India have taught me that direct and sustained eye contact with an elder is considered disrespectful. The question is, now that our world is so globally connected, how do we manage these cultural differences? The first is to become educated about them, so that, for example, if someone refuses to make eye contact, you can determine whether or not it is due to his or her culture. The second is not to impose your cultural bias outward, but to be respectful and patient with the signals you receive. This can be challenging, but it is worth its weight in gold for building trust.

In our increasingly global world and given that eye contact is viewed very differently by various cultures, it is vital to familiarize yourself with the traditions of the people with whom you may be working. Everyone has to be flexible, to bend a bit around the extremes of cultural behaviors. But keep in mind, other people are coming from their own "unconscious" muscle memory and may not be able to "feel" in their muscles how their eyes are communicating. It is equally important not to project your values onto someone from another culture for whom direct eye contact may be considered rude or disrespectful. Find out as best as you can the traditions of someone from a foreign culture before "interpreting" his or her body language from *your* frame of reference. Keep an open mind and listen not merely to the eyes, words, and face, but take in the entire being as he or she communicates. We send an infinity of messages in a multitude of ways far beyond the most obvious. It takes time and attention to be able to read people to the best of our ability. And even then, at best, we are mostly guessing! Nonetheless, I have found that by not imposing any imperative for eye contact and just being patient, in time even the most reluctant, guarded eye contact seems to fade away, irrespective of culture or gender.

The greater challenge for those who tend not to make eye contact is that they miss seeing the microsignals coming their way. When eyes are focused down, up, or away for long periods of time, they can't capture what's visually being expressed toward them. To miss those signals can have serious results. Whether driven by culture or habit, it's important to understand the impact that not making eye contact can have on any encounter and work toward finding a happy medium.

To make sufficient eye contact, however, doesn't mean to stare. Eye contact that's maintained 60 to 70 percent of the time is sufficient to signal your presence and attention. Also, we've all sat in meetings where the person in charge focuses exclusively on one or two people, thereby making those excluded from eye contact feel "lesser." (Never forget: today's junior may be tomorrow's president. Honor *everyone*.)

TRY THIS: STAR EYES

Rent a movie and, with the sound turned off, watch to see if you can guess the emotional content from the actors' eyes. You'll note quick and constant changes in the muscles around the eyes.

The length of eye contact, smiling with the eyes to signal agreement, quick darting eye movements from side to side—there are an infinite number of signals that the eyes send, and if they are not within your conscious control, there can be serious consequences. One client who was being groomed for a promotion had the habit of darting his eyes quickly to the left while he framed answers to questions. It was an unconscious habit with no overt intention, but the effect on his observers was profound. This rapid, habitual, unconscious movement made him appear unsure and, to some, untrustworthy. This couldn't have been farther from the truth! He was an entirely capable, honest, and completely above-board fellow, but this unconscious habit was a serious hindrance to his success. When I pointed it out, he had no idea what I was talking about. He literally could not even feel it. When he saw himself on video, he was shocked.

"It's so obvious. I can't believe I do that, and I had no idea. I look so shifty-eyed." We worked on it by having him do the shifting movement on purpose. We slowly broke down the gesture into tiny increments so that he could consciously feel and isolate the muscles at the very beginning of the movement. Only by forcing himself to "consciously" shift his eyes could he train his brain to recognize the feeling and break the habit.

While it seems counterintuitive, I've found this approach of slowly and intentionally repeating a habitual, unconscious, potentially derailing gesture so that it can be consciously "felt" to be quite successful. I've used it with chronic eyebrow raisers, those who carry a lot of brow tension, as well as stomach and shoulder grippers. When muscles move in certain ways for decades, they literally become stuck in patterns that can no longer be sensed and the brain seems unable to recognize. They become automatic. (The more any gesture is repeated, the deeper the neural paths associated with it.) But by applying slow-motion movement with focused awareness, these habits can be identified and broken.

TRY THIS: JUST AN INCH!

For a simple way to experience just how profoundly muscle memory is embedded in the body, try walking with your feet turned in or out just and inch, or shorten or lengthen your gait by just a few inches. It will feel massively different. That's how powerful muscle memory is.

TRY THIS: HABIT BREAKER

If you become aware of any unconscious physical habit, break it down into its microelements, very slowly repeating them with conscious focus and intention. This will allow the brain to register it and begin to catch it before it catches you. This is not something to be done merely once or twice, but repeatedly over time, sometimes for weeks or months. For old habits to be broken and new ones to be created takes tremendous focus and attention.

TRY THIS: MIRROR TALK

Watch yourself in the mirror while talking on the phone. Observe how the head sits on the neck, what the mouth does, and how muscles around the eyes move as you talk about various subjects. Observe how the intention of the communication succeeds or is hindered by any habitual muscular movement. Once conscious of any habitual derailers, you can begin to address them through the repetition exercise suggested above. For even more information, video-record your face while communicating.

FACE NEUTRAL

Somewhere between a blank stare and an easily readable expression sits face neutral. Relaxed, open, listening, face neutral does not reveal your emotional response. It is present but not judgmental, acute but not worried. It is accomplished by relaxing the muscles from brow to jaw, keeping the lips closed but not pressed together. Why have this expression at your disposal? Several reasons. There are times when it is essential to signal our emotional response with our faces, and there are times when, for a myriad of reasons, it's counterproductive to reveal our emotions. Managers, teachers, or even parents, as they listen to two sides of a story, should attempt to be open to both sides. Practicing a neutral facial expression will not signal bias as you listen, and thus it will not reveal your emotions and reactions to the speaker. During negotiations, employing face neutral is often essential. (Teenagers are masters of face neutral when they don't want their parents to know something is up!)

EARS

Listening is my personal obsession (and passion) because I encounter very few people who truly embrace and understand what listening asks of us. Listening is an art that requires training. Unfortunately, despite the fact that how we listen affects everything we do, there is no curriculum designed to teach listening. *How* we listen has a direct result on *what* we hear, and *what* we hear often has an imme-diate impact on *how* we react. Our reactions then set up other reactions, often in microseconds, and before we know it, an emotional avalanche is under way.

Listening requires muscle, stillness, calm, and . . . wisdom. There are also many levels to listening and to listening with openness. There is literal listen-ing to the sounds around you, with conscious attention. Most of us tune out the myriad of sounds that occur moment by moment, but a good way to begin to address active, or empathic, listening is not to tune out sounds but to become so still as to really absorb them.

TRY THIS: ELEPHANT EARS

Sit in a chair, close your eyes, follow your breath for a few moments, and then tune *into* sound. First pay attention to the sounds that are immediately around you: your breath, a clock ticking, the radiator hissing. Then expand your consciousness to the sounds immediately outside the room you are in. Keep expanding down the hall, outside the building, in nature—just keep expanding your listening so that your entire body becomes an enormous ear. You'll be amazed at how both relaxing and energizing this small exercise can be. Rather than shutting out sound, you begin to seek it out eagerly, and it is always full of rich surprises.

Even on the purely physical level, listening is a delicious moment-to-moment encounter with the world around us. As noise levels increase everywhere, we rou-tinely try to shut out sound or plug our ears with headphones. Unless you're in an environment that is painfully noisy, actively listening to the richness of sound is a delight in its own right. Tuning in rather than tuning out is fascinating. I once knew a drummer who rode the subway just to listen to the varying rhythms created by the tracks. So much of what we try to avoid, if we merely relax and let it in, reduces stress enormously.

This exercise is both a pleasure and a warm-up to a deeper kind of listening. After practicing this level of listening to the "outer" stimuli, begin to focus inward and listen to yourself. The first muscle required to enable active and open listening to others is the ability to hear oneself, to step away from one's thinking process or the endless loops of inner noise that consume vast amounts of our mental energy.

INSIDE THE HEAD: LISTENING INSIDE AND RESPONDING OUT

Many of us don't think; we obsess or ruminate. We have repeated conversations with those who are not present, either rehearsing some future encounter, replaying a past one, or *rewriting* one already experienced. We spend vast amounts of time locked inside our heads with little conscious connection to the moment in which we are actually living. But how we think has a direct impact on how we behave and who we become. The *Dhammapada Sutra* famously says, "We are what we think." Many meditation practices are designed as a way to step beyond that constant inner noise to the deeper, quieter self. That deeper self has been given many names: the third eye, the watcher, true being, Buddha Nature. It is essentially that part of *isness* that is beyond the chronic, habitual, busy, thinking mind most of us occupy most of the time. It is a place of stillness and involved detachment. By listening hard to our own thinking process, we begin to discover that aspect of being that isn't "attached" to endless loops of obsession. We can actually begin to hear our own nonsense, how passionately involved it is with either defending ourselves, judging others or ourselves, critiquing, or assessing. We are all geniuses of righteousness or masterminds of self-loathing. What we aren't are skilled observers of ourselves.

Listening to our thoughts and then watching them go by is the first step toward connecting with that part of the self that goes beyond the ego's need to be right, or better, or the best. We can enter a place of stillness and calm that offers perspective and even relief. This is not to say that all thinking is bad or wasteful. Thinking is an excellent tool when it is applied to solving problems, managing complexity, creating alternatives. But that kind of focused thinking is the opposite of the endless, ruminating mind chatter that obliterates our ability to be fully here in the now. Why is this important for communication? Because it's impossible to connect when we're stuck in our own heads and not tuned into the moment.

TRY THIS: INNER EAR

After doing the "Elephant Ears" exercise for a few minutes, shift your attention to what is happening inside your head. First listen to sound and then listen to your thoughts. By doing so, you can begin to develop an inner ear that hears thoughts beyond the most obvious, the equivalent of the silence between the notes in music. Most meditation is about "letting go" of thoughts, and that is a great practice. But there is great value as well in actively listening to the constant inner chatter. Themes that run as a quiet constant inside the mind can be observed. Do they have value? Are they aligned with the actual present, or are they vestigial habits, old voices? The simple truth is, if you don't hear them, you can't modify them.

At work, those more adept at quieting the inner chatter have an easier time really hearing others. Often when listening we're (a) waiting for the speaker to get to the point, (b) judging, (c) criticizing, (d) assessing, (e) deciding if we agree or not, (f) planning our rebuttal, (g) processing how to respond. Sound familiar? Very few people merely listen. Encountering those who manage to shut off their own inner tapes and truly enter a place of pure listening is wonderful and inspiring. Their power and effectiveness are often a direct result of their listening style. Also those who feel deeply heard, even when there are conflicting points of view in response to their ideas, are far more open to navigating those conflicting responses. Being heard creates a powerful bond. Bonds build trust; trust builds relationships; relationships build business. It all starts with and hinges on deep listening.

There are also concrete ways, once one shuts off the inner tapes and truly listens, to signal that one is fully present. Eye contact, as mentioned earlier, allows you as a listener to receive microsignals. The best way to listen is to completely stop what you are doing. Put down that smartphone or close that spreadsheet and turn to face the speaker. Using your upper torso, not just your head, face the person and look in his or her eyes. While the person is speaking, quiet your thoughts and listen not just to the words and tone but to the whole body—

the gestures, posture, and facial expressions. Listen as well to that which is not said but is expressed emotionally. As you listen, signal to the speaker that you hear him or her by occasionally nodding and smiling. You can nod even if you disagree with the content, because nodding doesn't signal accord, merely understanding and presence. (Beware of too much nodding, however, as that can send a signal that you are overly in agreement when that may not be the case. Additionally, too much nodding can actually impact your own decision making. If working globally, familiarize yourself with the different cultural meanings of nodding. For example, in India nodding means I hear you, not I agree with you.)

These are such basic rules of engagement that it's amazing to me how often people forget them. There are so many things pulling on our attention, competing for our time, that we forget the power of simply stopping and listening.

Responding after listening is another skill that requires stillness. Many clients have said, "But if I take time to actually think about my response, I'll be perceived as ignorant, weak, or unsure." This is a symptom of how communication has been affected by lightning-speed technology. Thinking is not a sign of stupidity or weakness! It's exactly the opposite. Taking the time to frame, shape, and think through a response indicates not only security but the ability to weigh alternatives.

If, when listening, you give your full attention both physically and mentally to the speaker, if you quiet your busy mind and become as empty as possible, you can more easily access a part of yourself that is beyond the immediacy of the situation at hand. You can actually tap into wisdom as opposed to mere information or defensiveness. I can imagine the multitudes of heads shaking. *Who needs wisdom when the boss wants to know the numbers for the third-quarter bottom line!* Practical nuts-and-bolts answers, when asked for, are one thing. But sometimes the kinds of questions posed in complex communication are far less cut and dried. They are open-ended and require thought. When we rush to answer as a way to demonstrate how "on top if it" we are, we often reveal the exact opposite. Remember, a question can be asked for a multitude of reasons—for the information the seeker doesn't have, for your opinion, as a test, to poke holes in your argument—to name just a few. By really hearing the question, and *what lies underneath*, you can answer from a much more intelligent place. If you just jump in without thought, you can miss addressing the deeper question. Whether the question comes from a peer, client, or boss, at root, most questions are, "Can you solve my problem?" "How?" "By when?" "Why not?" At the bottom of what may appear to be aggressive digging for answers is often anxiety. The questioner needs your answer, hopes it's right, fears you may not know it either. When responding from a place of calm listening, you are supplying not only the contextual answer the person may want but also the subtextual need he or she feels.

When what you have said is challenged or triggers actual aggression, the tendency is to defend. Listening stops, and points are lobbed back and forth with increasing intensity. A better practice is to respond to aggressive questions with curiosity. When someone overtly disagrees, take a breath and ask the person to explain in a bit more detail what the reservations are. Really listen to what is provided. As it becomes clearer why he or she may disagree, try, without getting defensive, to take in the new information being offered. To make sure you really understand, use the person's precise words as you repeat the core difference or challenge that's been expressed. Then don't stop there; keep drilling down. "So, if I understand you correctly, you think this idea cannot work because . . . ?" Curiosity, along with drilling down and reflecting back, can defuse problematic exchanges and even create new solutions. But you've got to *really* listen.

POINT OF VIEW

> *"It is hard to fight an enemy*
> *who has outposts in your head."*
>
> —SALLY KEMPTON

I worked with a senior vice president at a multinational corporation who suffered from stage fright. Her fear of presenting was so crippling that she actually scheduled vacations to coincide with major town hall presentations. Days before a presentation, she'd be unable to sleep; hours before, she'd begin to sweat, shake, and then become so dry in the mouth that she could hardly speak. As we worked together, I asked her to tell me what she imagined audiences think about her. In a blink she replied, "That I'm not good enough. That I don't deserve this position." This was her belief, despite her success and her having been in her current position for some time.

The other belief she had was that mistakes are failures.

When I suggested that mistakes are quite human, everyone makes them, they're often not the end of the world, and quite frequently they can be portals to discovery, she looked at me like I was completely insane. Our "belief" systems were in direct opposition. What my comment permitted her to consider, however, was that this belief was merely that, a belief, not the truth.

What happens with these kinds of beliefs is that once we become convinced of them, we experience them as true. Then they can become self-fulfilling prophesies. By consciously exploring deeply ingrained beliefs that impact our emotional reaction system—and our bodies—we can begin to craft different patterns of thought and emotional response. This is not merely shifting the glass from half empty to half full, or the power of positive thinking, but consciously exploring the deep habitual ways we signal and send messages to ourselves, thereby creating certain patterns and outcomes. By consciously shifting those signals, we can create profoundly different outcomes and impact.

In theater, the term *point of view* is used instead of *belief*. But it's very similar. If two actors are rehearsing the balcony scene from *Romeo and Juliet*, they learn the lines, the movement, and blocking (where they will move on stage). They decide on the actions they'll play in order to fulfill their objectives. Romeo's objective is to get Juliet to fall in love with him, despite the history of the family feud. His actions might be to woo, or to convince, or to impress. To make an actor's choice more intricate or subtle, a director might say to Romeo, "OK, it's coming along. This time I'd like you to do it with the point of view, or inner secret or belief: 'I never get what I want.'"

That choice, that subtle inner belief, will totally color how Romeo plays the scene. It will, in theater terms, "read." Likewise, if the director gives the actor the note, "Try it this time and play with the point of view 'I'm irresistible,'" imagine the difference. Suddenly, the actor will have an entirely new air about him, cocky, sure, sexy, arrogant. It's difficult to predict, but the only certainty is that the inner thought will have a profound effect on the signals sent, on the body that sends them, and upon the receiver.

Why is that? Point of view is powerful. When an actor shifts his point of view from "I never get what I want" to "I'm irresistible," the effect on his carriage, movements, facial expression, voice, pace, confidence, attractiveness—to name just a few—shifts dramatically. Point of view is not merely playing with opposites, but exploring and having fun with nuance. For one actor, that point of view might open up a whole new vein of impulses and ideas. For another, it might go nowhere. Part of the game and joy of playing with point of view comes from the unpredictable and unintended results.

Going into a meeting you're dreading? A job interview that puts your stomach in a knot? You can think over and over, "I'm so dreading this. I never know what to say," or instead flip your point of view. Try "I'm going to be the best possible candidate." "I can't wait to see whom I might meet." "I'm so curious about what will happen." Why not? Point of view aligned with a clear intention, "I'm going to learn something new at this meeting or event," can radically shift your experience and the outcome. Taking the time to notice habitual, negative, limiting points of view and craft alternatives requires awareness and time.

TRY THIS: TAKE A THOUGHT FOR A WALK

Ready to play? Pick a fun, even wacky, point of view and go do an errand. Here are a few to play with: "I'm gorgeous!" "Everybody loves me." "Nothing scares me." "Awesome day!" "I always get what I want." Go to the grocery store or the bank. Walk around and see how it influences what you observe, how you communicate, and how others respond to you.

I once was at a conference where I'd been the keynote speaker the day before. I was in a terrible rush to make a flight, but it would have been very rude if upon entering the conference center I didn't stop to speak to people who wanted to ask me questions. I picked the point of view that I was invisible. Actually, I went farther than that and decided I was clear. I focused on that for a few moments, tucked my head down, pulled up my shirt collar, hoped attendees would be in meetings. Much to my surprise, I discovered that they were all on break. "I'm clear, totally clear; they cannot see me" was all I thought over and over. No one saw me. Not one person . . . because I was clear! (Or maybe just see-through!)

Day in and day out, each of us has no end of choices of how to deal with the challenges ahead. How often do we choose our thoughts in a direct and immediate way? In the present moment? We can practice shifting our habitual thinking patterns moment by moment. We can practice the cessation of thinking (which, for most, is merely obsessing over the same tired worries), being present in the moment and harnessing our powers to solve problems and create new inventions. We can consciously shift our point of view as we would consciously solve a math problem.

The beauty of shifting our point of view is that the results are immediate. An altered point of view will quickly be integrated by the body. If one consciously chooses the point of view "I'm excited to see what's going to happen" and then pairs it briefly with the physical gesture of happy clapping hands, even just for a few seconds, the emotional body will quickly begin to shift. A shift from, "I'm terrifed I'll mess up," to "Everything will be fine," coupled with arms raised in victory and repeatedly whispered "Yes! Yes! Yes!" can change you and the outcome.

Actors do these sorts of things all the time as a way of preparing for an entrance. How does an actor make the audience believe he's just come inside from a raging snowstorm when everyone knows he's just entered from backstage? He brings the cold in with him by doing all manner of physical gestures that conjure up the weather outside and its effects on his body. And not just the weather but what happened to him before he came on. Did he run into his beloved? Did he have an argument with a neighbor? Whatever emotional and physical experience he encountered before entering the stage must be embodied so it rings true and is communicated clearly. The same practices could be employed by nonactors were they taught the means to do so.

Sometimes I suggest to those who worry about how they're perceived or who have impostor syndrome that they try on the point of view "I'm a subject expert," "I'm the best," or "I really know my stuff." Or as with Clair in the Introduction, "I'm queen." Often they'll counter that that's egocentric or too "showy." And I agree that using that point of view as a way to get attention for oneself will indeed come off as egocentric. But to be a subject expert *in service* to an organization is not making it all about you; it's about making you more effective for the workplace, so that you have the confidence to deliver what's needed. On the other hand, with those who are arrogant and quite full of themselves, I suggest they try the point of view "How can I help?" "What *don't* I know?" And for those who are stressed to the maximum and feel that the entire organization will fall apart if they take a sick day, I ask them to take a few deep breaths, imagine a walk on the beach, and say the point of view "It'll be OK" or even "So what?" The results are invariably amazing.

FRAME SHIFT

The operative word here is *play*. We take ourselves so seriously. We move in the same limited repetitive ways day in and day out. Yet we have so many options. How rarely, past the age of 9 or 10, do we actually play? Play for adults is confined to sports, video games, crossword puzzles, dinner parties, or the occasional concert, dance performance, or art exhibit. But opportunities for play are available every moment of the day.

TRY THIS: WORD MOVE

Take a piece of paper and tear it into one-inch strips. Write down a word on each strip; choose any random words but preferably nouns. Fold up the pieces of paper and toss them into a bowl. Stand up. Relax. Take a few deep breaths. Shake out a bit. Pick one of the folded strips of paper, open it, and read the word. Without any thought, as quickly as possible, let the body instantly react to the word by making a grand movement or gesture that expresses your reaction to that word. Relax. Pick another word. React. And another. Observe the thoughts that come into your head as you do this.

I'll repeat that: *Observe the thoughts that come into your head as you do this.*

Note the judge, that voice that puts this exercise down as foolish, embarrassing, or infantile. We ridicule play. We find it wasteful and unproductive. It doesn't *make* anything. It just is. Of course, it is the very *isness* of play that is so valuable. To play, one must be able to surrender to the moment, to give in to whatever happens next without trying to control it. To just be. What thoughts came to you as you attempted this exercise, if indeed you allowed yourself to do it? How loud were those thoughts that "judged" you? Were you able to ignore them, or did they stop you in your tracks? What were the precise words that came to you? Did they sound familiar? Have you heard them before? I'll bet you have. And here's the kicker—why do they have any validity at all? Why do we listen to the self-sabotaging judge when all it does is stop us from playing and stepping beyond the limits it sets? Who made the judge the arbiter of what is permissible?

There is a difference between the self-sabotaging judge and the socialized mature adult: the former is a joy-killing internal voice, and the latter is essential for society and the workplace to function. We inherit all these limits, set well before we had any say in the matter. But then we carry them inside for the *rest of our lives*, often without questioning them. But the all-knowing judge—that punishing inner voice that criticizes with such impunity—is very different from the observant self, and the two should not be confused with each other. The judge is a killer. It kills spontaneity, joy, play, impulse, risk. It's wedded to shame, ego, pride, and guilt. If you live in its shadow, it always wins. Even if it only crops up occasionally, you cannot win a fight with the judge. You cannot negotiate with the judge. It lives in a part of the self that is so ancient and rooted to early childhood unconscious memory that at best all you can do is recognize it and attempt, as best you can, to ignore it.

TRY THIS: OUT LOUD

Pick another word out of the bowl, read it, gesture, and say out loud all the things the judge is saying about you or the exercise. By saying the words of the judge out loud, you can actually hear those words and begin to distance yourself from the judge and observe how it limits risk taking on so many levels.

You may think, "I can't play like that. I can't be inappropriately silly. I have to be professional, reliable, and mature." Certainly one can't be inappropriately silly in a business setting. But what the unconscious, global judge does is limit us *everywhere*. It just doesn't pipe up occasionally. It seeps into our daily life and saps creativity and fun at every juncture. It haunts us. Those who operate under the judge's orders never break free. They second-guess what they want to say in meetings; they cut off their creativity, refuse risk, and avoid the new. People for whom the judge is ever present are terrified of failure, embarrassment, and humiliation, so they operate within very routine, confined, safe borders. Interestingly, certain businesses and corporations actively use this fear to their advantage and attract employees who, despite great intelligence and talent, are terribly risk averse. Not very fun places to work. Is that how your place of business operates? Is that what initially attracted you? Is that where you wish to stay?

By trying "Word Move" and "Out Loud," you're providing yourself the opportunity to isolate and hear the judge in a controlled and safe setting. Only by objectively hearing and isolating its overtly critical voice can you begin to drop it. And that is all one can do, because you cannot negotiate or win a fight with the judge. It will always win. Dropping it, like discarding heavy luggage that weighs you down, is the only choice. How?

TRY THIS: JUDGE'S JOURNAL

To grow muscles that are aligned with the part of the self that is not identified with the judge—muscles indifferent to external ideas of "success" or "being right," muscles that take you into the moment and beyond "results"—it's important to identify the specificity of your own personal judge. One of the best ways to do this is to write down what the judge actually says. Buy a small diary and carry it with you. As you notice what the judge says, write it down. Get it out of your head and onto a piece of paper. Externalize it. Carry the notebook everywhere for several weeks and jot down random judge comments and thoughts. *Don't reread the comments or the journal.*

TRY THIS: JUDGE'S JOURNAL REPLIES

After a few weeks of making entries, sit down and read the entire judge's journal. Do you notice certain themes? What are they? Bucket together all those that fit into clear themes and title the themes. Now write down an alternative thought to what the judge says. If, for example, a constant theme is "You're not smart enough," what might you reply to that? "I didn't get this far by being stupid." Or "There are many kinds of intelligence." Or "I can learn what I don't know." Write those down in a new journal. Finding an alternative to the ever-critical judge is the first step to getting out from under its destructiveness. As you train yourself to find alternative thoughts and ignore the judge, you'll begin to discover how much more creative, fun, and successful your day becomes. This is a frame shift, literally turning a thought upside-down so that you can see the world differently.

Why write by hand? Why not do it on computer? One reason for writing in a small diary is privacy. Another, it can always be tucked in a pocket and carried with you. But most importantly, handwriting slows us down. It uses gestures that are deeply ingrained in our neural circuitry. Handwriting allows for a deeper connection to what is experienced. It creates a quiet self-communion that a keyboard cannot provide.

IMAGINATION

When I discussed point of view with a client, she remarked, "In golf it's called the swing thought." Her golf pro had taught her to actively imagine the golf swing in her mind's eye before she physically did it, to visualize first the swing and then the trajectory the ball would take. Mind maps of habitual movements that help us to predict where the body needs to go happen automatically. The intentional visualization of a physical act is a bit different and is a discipline. It needs to be practiced as much as the physical act of actually swinging the golf club. But it needn't be just for sports or movement. One can visualize any number of things before a meeting, a presentation, or any high-stakes communication. Often, due to stress, we tend to imagine the worst. But with a little bit of effort, changing the movie inside the mind can alter the eventual outcome.

Before your next high-stakes presentation, don't allow your imagination to hurl you down a path of negatives—typically, "What if I forget my words or lose my place?" As a matter of fact, this is the most common anxiety I encounter. It's *OK*. *Everyone* forgets words. Just roll with it. If during a presentation you do forget a word, say aloud, "Oh, what's the word I'm thinking of?" You'll be amazed by how sympathetic people will be, sometimes even supplying the missing word for you! Sometimes people worry about blushing or shaking. To blush is to be. It's your passion expressing itself and is nothing to be ashamed of. *Own* it! Also, amazingly, when people stress about blushing or blotching, and I've coached them to "love their blush," it has sometimes completely disappeared. Regarding shaking, there are exercises provided later on that help to ground the arms and legs. The key thought here is to create a different mental image of the outcome.

TRY THIS: STANDING O

Before a high-stakes presentation or meeting, imagine instead your body is a rooted, tall, very strong tree that is grounded and secure. Imagine the audience giving you a standing ovation and calling out "Bravo!" It's almost guaranteed that won't happen, but it is a preferable vision to help you launch your talk and dispel the natural anxiety that comes with any big presentation than the typical ones driven by fear. You may even enter the meeting with excitement instead of dread!

So much happens inside the head. In order to connect, it's vital to understand the degree to which your physical body aligns with your thoughts to create the bonds that will allow you to succeed. Recent studies suggest that meditation, long demonstrated to reduce stress and promote calm and well-being, can also train attention itself. For a long time, attentional blink, a brain phenomenon where things happen far too fast for the brain to detect, was thought to be a fixed, immutable property of the nervous system. But it's been determined that attention itself is a skill that can be enhanced, trained, and increased. It is not fixed at all but actually quite flexible. Increasingly, we are learning that what we believed to be immutable is utterly fluid; it is merely our perception that is stuck. Recent research into intelligence is demonstrating that it too is plastic and can change and grow. The notion of a fixed IQ may soon enter the dustbin of history!

The same can be said of the judge. Habitually negative points of view restrict the imagination. As deeply ingrained and habit-driven as we are, with practice, focus, and attention, habitual thoughts can be shifted. They can be modified so as not to work against you, but *for* you. Precisely because our emotions are so contagious, playing with these kinds of mental and physical shifts can also greatly benefit those with whom we interact and alter the social sphere and scripts in which we live and work.

Chapter 1: Use Your Head

Speaking/Posture

- **Happy/Sad Mouth**—emotion-body feedback loop
- **Sweet Apricot: Jaw Relax**—jaw tension
- **Head Hinge**—subtext from head position
- **Broken Bridge**—emotion-body feedback loop, posture
- **Wet Dog**—relaxation, voice-body connection
- **Head Hinge with Voice**—throat tension–head position impact on voice
- **Reverse Turtle Neck**—posture, proper head placement, voice

Seeing

- **Star Eyes**—eye communication
- **Just an Inch!**—muscle memory/habit
- **Habit Breaker**—micro-movements, unconscious habits
- **Mirror Talk**—observe unconscious habits

Listening

- **Elephant Ears**—focus, relaxation, listening
- **Inner Ear**—focus, attention, thought observation

Thinking

- **Take a Thought for a Walk**—thought-emotion-body feedback loop
- **Word Move**—identify inhibitors/impulse work, observe judge
- **Out Loud**—observe/separate from judge
- **Judge's Journal**—externalize the judge
- **Judge's Journal Replies**—create alternative modes of thinking
- **Standing O**—imagination, positive self-coaching

Exercise Name	Frequency Goal / Actual	Observations	Next Steps
Take a Thought for a Walk	2x per week	Gave me energy	Will do before next presentation
	/		
	/		
	/		
	/		
	/		

Have a Heart

*"When the heart speaks,
the mind finds it indecent to object."*
—MILAN KUNDERA

The first few minutes of my initial coaching session with Bruce progressed in a straightforward and typical fashion. I introduced myself and told him how I work and asked what he was hoping to achieve from the engagement. He discussed his challenges in running meetings and getting traction from his reports. "There's just so much resistance, and people always have excuses as to why they're not doing what I ask."

We discussed his background, and as he spoke, I noticed certain themes: how goal-driven he was, how he'd never before experienced so much oppositional behavior, how successful he'd always been—in school, sports, and business. How humble he wasn't! When I spoke, he interrupted, contradicted, or ignored what I had to say. When he wasn't speaking verbally, his body was speaking volumes: a shaking foot, a quick dismissive shake of the head, a downward curl of his lips. At one point, I gave up attempting to get through and decided to just hold my tongue and observe. At the end of this first meeting, I removed the DVD that had been recording our conversation and held it out to him.

"Well, Bruce. This has been an enlightening session for me, as I can see why you are encountering so much opposition."

"Yeah? Why's that?"

"Well, for one, you interrupted me every time I spoke, cutting me off mid-sentence with defensive, self-justifying arguments. Secondly, your behavior is smug, self-satisfied, and arrogant, and I've no doubt you are making the people who report to you feel insignificant and belittled."

Without a word Bruce snatched the DVD from my hand and stormed out of my office.

People tell me I tell it like I see it, which can be good or bad, depending . . . But I'd made a decision when I "told" it to Bruce, and it was calculated. On one hand, his behavior was truly obnoxious—arrogant, defensive, and self-righteous. On the other, he was scared, and I knew it. I also knew that I really didn't want to waste my time with someone who truly believed he had nothing to learn and was there merely to check off a box on his performance review. I called out to his retreating back, "If you've got the balls, watch the video."

My heart was going like a rocket in my chest. I'd done something I almost never do; I aggressed on a client. I was as hostile and nasty to him as he'd been to me. My very words went against everything I hold dear about my work, which is to approach all with an open heart. I work constantly not to judge but to listen. I'd broken every rule in my book. I'd said those things not to be mean, but in attempt to crack open his defenses and, I hoped, hold up a mirror to how he'd treated me and clearly was treating others. I knew I'd taken a big risk and perhaps a regrettable one, but I'd trusted my gut, and as much as I disliked his behavior, I still was coming from a good-hearted place. I assumed that would be the last time I'd see Bruce.

Three weeks later my phone rang. When my assistant told me it was he, I was quite surprised and prepared myself for the inevitable harangue. "This is Gina," I said coolly.

"Bruce here."

"Hello. How are you?"

"I just wanted to tell you something." I took a breath to prepare myself. "I have never been spoken to the way you spoke to me. For weeks I was furious, and actually fantasized about hurting you physically and professionally." There was a pregnant pause. I waited. "And then I looked at the videotape."

"And?" I asked

"Who would *ever* want to work for that asshole?" Bruce replied. "When can I see you again?"

"Wow," I replied. "What courage for you to call and tell me this! That's fantastic, Bruce. I'd be thrilled to keep working with you." And it was true. And here's the amazing thing: when that man walked into my office a few days later, his *eyes* were literally transformed. We went on to do amazing work together, and he grew into a person I deeply cared about, admired, and even loved.

Having a heart means coming from a place of generosity and giving, but that does not mean being protective of another's defenses. Always respect defenses, as they are deep-rooted and embedded for complicated reasons. But respect comes in many forms, and if you come from a place of genuine caring, you can say difficult things to people, in the hope of genuinely connecting. Again, it is important to be truthful regarding how your biases impact your "opinions" about others.

Defenses and defensiveness live as powerfully in the body as they do in behavior. People who feel compelled to defend themselves, who perceive differing opinions as assaults, embody a posture that will protect against those perceived assaults. They can carry excessive neck and shoulder tension (often accompanied by clenched jaws, furrowed brows, and tight forearms). Ready to spring into action to "defend," they are taut all over. Such habitually high-strung protective posture creates rigidity; as goes the body, so goes the mind. As with all personal histories, defensiveness may be a chicken-or-egg situation. Is someone defensive because of early childhood trauma? Perhaps. Assaults or insults experienced when 3, 9, or 15 are ancient history and no longer present. And yet by having the body and the subconscious continue to carry and exhibit that history, defensive types often *re-create situations in the present* that mirror those early childhood traumas. This then keeps the need for defensiveness alive. The cycle is complete. How to break that cycle via the body and an open heart is what we'll explore.

THE HEART

When an actor prepares for a role, he or she may write an imaginary autobiography of the character. The actor does this to dig into the historic underbelly of what might have made the character behave as he or she does. This exercise is particularly useful when playing a villain. The actor needs a backstory to explain the character's dangerous or outright hateful actions because the job of every actor is to play the character with full commitment and no judgment.

To fully embody an "other," an actor must suspend his or her opinions on the character. No one thinks he's a bad guy. Essentially, people believe what they think and do is right, and it's the other guy who is ill-informed or biased. That's how we are. By writing an autobiography, the actor is opening his heart to the character in a way that doesn't excuse bad behavior but seeks to unravel the mystery of its causation. Might one be able to do this in the workplace? Might a nonactor be able to imaginatively step into the mind, heart, and soul of another?

When I teach my corporate communications workshops, I sometimes ask clients to close their eyes and imagine someone they deeply admire, either from their personal or work life or from public life, history, or even fiction. As they think of that person, I ask them to imagine his or her voice, the way that person moves, gestures, listens, laughs. I ask them to picture the person's hair, shoes, hands. Usually within seconds there is a subtle but absolutely discernible shift in how the client is breathing, sitting, and just "being." Why? Because the client has an open heart to that individual and can allow that essence to be manifest within him or her. I sometimes then ask the client to present or converse with me not "as" the character, but as the imagined character "might" communicate. The transformation is immediate. Still oneself, but having permission to embody someone deeply admired, something amazing happens. It's as though the client's insides shift. The heart is open to that admirable person and thus to that part of the self, to the aspirations one holds for oneself. My question is, can we not do this with everyone? Must we only be able to open our hearts to those who mirror our own values? Can we not open our hearts to all?

TRY THIS: EMBODIED ASPIRATION

Imagine someone you deeply love or admire. Close your eyes and picture that person as fully as possible—his or her walk, voice, gestures. Open your eyes and walk around your home or apartment as him or her. What do you notice? How do your thoughts change? How do you move?

TRY THIS: EMBODIED ICK

Now let's do the exact same exercise with someone you dislike or even loathe. Imagine the person so thoroughly that you can briefly become him or her. What happens?

If you gave yourself permission to do the above, excellent! What did you discover?

It is well understood that people repeatedly re-create the same dysfunctional patterns: they'll date people who on the surface seem wildly different but underneath are practically interchangeable; they'll jump from job to job but invariably find the same "impossible" boss. *Repetition compulsion* is a psychological term, but it lives in the body as well. The frequent result? When a body is chronically defensive, it often attracts aggression. While it's not irrelevant how, when, or even why the defensiveness originated, what is crucial is the recognition that it lives on in the body and through the body. Anxiety, fear, self-judgment—all of these find a home in the body.

What is an open heart? How can having an open heart impact your ability to connect, listen, or lead? Will an open heart make you weak or vulnerable? A target? Too easily swayed? A pushover? How can you balance an open heart with difficult and often painful decision making? How can you achieve an open heart toward someone you passionately dislike or disagree with?

Years ago, studies found that doctors who had made bad clinical decisions and had terrible bedside manners were sued for malpractice with much greater frequency than doctors who'd made the same level of clinical errors but who had good patient relations. Patients were far more hesitant to sue the doctors they liked and who they felt "cared" for them, irrespective of the doctors' grievous errors. Why would someone whose life was put in serious jeopardy by a bad medical decision not seek recompense merely because the doctor had a good bedside manner? Because everyone makes mistakes, but coming from a genuine place of concern clearly makes those mistakes more forgivable. Why? Because we are emotional beings. We are relationship beings. We build trust through our interactions, our behaviors, how we listen, and how we lead. Welcoming any person with an open heart, and by that I mean nonjudgmental, respectful acceptance of the person's unique self, requires the willingness to let go of one's own sense of righteousness.

How to do that? Behavior, the product of numerous factors—history, upbringing, family, genetics, ideology, to name a few—is enormously influenced as well by self-conception. There are self-proclaimed experts who feel no need to define nor defend the decisions they make. "I'm right" is more than sufficient. But self-conception itself is a tricky and moving target. One day you wake up feeling "I'm a super hotshot," the next "I'm a lowly worm." Both may be true and false. (Extremes on any end of the spectrum are highly suspect.) But true or false, fluid or static, how we think of ourselves greatly determines how we behave. These behaviors can be singular or collective. Collectively, in the Jim Crow era, whites thought they were better than blacks. Nazis thought Aryans were a superior race. The tzars of Russia thought they were demigods and behaved with ruthless impunity. As individuals, many people vacillate between superior and inferior self-conceptualizations. Supermodels will think they are gorgeous one day and hideous the next.

Self-conceptualization is also the result of numerous influences—language, culture, gender, family history, relationships, religion, and actual neural patterns. When the goal is to come from an open heart, toward oneself or toward others, one of the first steps is to identify how you self-conceptualize.

TRY THIS: THE LIST OF YOU (Part One)

Write a list of all the ways you think of yourself. All of them, the good, the bad, and the ugly. Don't do this in one sitting, but keep the list updated and alive for a week or two; and as you notice how you think of yourself, jot it down. Put the list away, and a couple of weeks later, give it a look. Ask yourself how many of the ways in which you think of yourself are based in reality, history, what your parents, siblings, teachers, classmates, friends, previous partners, spouses said about you. Identify which ways actually *serve your growth now as an evolving person*. How many are ancient, vestigial, inherited, out-of-date? If you created the judge journal as suggested in Chapter 1, do you see any parallels?

TRY THIS: THE LIST OF YOUR NEMESIS (Part Two)

Identify someone from work who *really* annoys you. Write down what about that person makes you angry. Put that list away. After a few days compare lists and see if there is any relationship between that person's negative traits and how you self-conceptualize. Frequently the most annoying behaviors in others mirror aspects of ourselves with which we also struggle. Those traits reflect the very things we dislike in ourselves, setting up a dissonance similar to two musical notes that don't mesh.

The first step in attempting to live with an open heart is to exhibit one toward yourself. We are all incredibly imperfect. We are all in a state of constant flux and change. We are all guilty of envy, rigidity, stubbornness, judgment, inferiority, superiority. No one is perfect, and no one is anything but a continuously changing, vulnerable, imperfect being of accumulated thoughts, habits, and behaviors. We are all living within our very private conception of reality and struggling to make some kind of meaning out of this random thing called existence.

We all know we're mortal, but few of us actually believe it. But if you live with the fact of your own mortality at the top of your mind day in and day out, it is virtually impossible not to feel your heart crack open. Life is so terribly brief! An open heart bypasses the labeling of oneself and others. It becomes where you start with people, not where you end up once you know them. It changes how you greet people and how you perceive their childish, ego-driven, faulty behaviors. As you accept and forgive your own frailties, those of others become far less irksome.

TRY THIS: OPEN HEART

Relax your shoulders completely. Float your head. Take a deep breath, close your eyes, and put all your awareness into the center of your chest. Let it soften and open. Whatever and whoever come to mind, soften the heart. Literally feel that part of the body get very, very soft and warm. Imagine it glowing, emitting a pale light. If any memory or upcoming stress comes to mind, just relax the heart. Keep breathing; keep softening; keep breathing; keep softening. See what that feels like. Notice, if tension creeps back in, where does it go? Soften the heart. Breathe. Soften the heart. Smile, not in a fake or forced way, but gently. Soften the heart. Melt the hardness away.

Can one do this at work? On the mean streets of a city? At the gym? Look around you in any of these places. Compassion, empathy, the ability to imagine an other, irrespective of whether or not you like the person, is the work of the heart. It is easy to love those whom you admire; it is hard to be open to those who deeply annoy and may even threaten you. But the latter are those who demand the leap of empathy.

If you really struggle with a colleague or manager with whom you simply cannot get along, ask yourself, at what age do you think that person is emotionally "arrested"? When I hear stories of dreadful office politics, the endless jockeying for power, attention, and real estate, I immediately think of junior high and that stage of maturation. Many professionals look and sound like adults, but scratch the surface and emotionally they are stuck at 3 years old, or 6, or 9, or—heaven forbid—13! It's undoubtedly a challenge to have a boss who possesses genius for an area of expertise but the emotional maturity of a 7-year-old. But understanding where someone may be stuck is the ticket to navigating that person's fragile ego and sense of self. Empathic intelligence, compassion, and open-heartedness are all admirable goals, but in truth they are where we must begin with each other. It takes work, but it is well worth the effort.

Sometimes, despite all we do, we simply cannot crack the code of someone's bad behavior, nor can we stop being reactive to it. What then? There are several options: Observe where your reaction goes in *your* body. Where do you get tense? Belly, chest, jaw, back, head? Develop the practice of noticing quickly and often how someone else's triggering behavior impacts *your* body. Does the person make you feel like you want to run away, duck and hide, or beat him or her up? Where does that impulse reside? In your legs, shoulders, arms? Once you notice what happens in your body, focus all your energy into calming and relaxing that area of reactive tension. Breathe; count to 10. Do nothing. Feel it. Just observe. Relax the areas and keep breathing into the tense areas, perhaps even softening them. By breaking your body's reactive habit, different, more tolerable responses to the person might emerge. If all else fails, it is time to make an honest assessment. *Behaviors can change, but personalities are pretty much fixed.* There are personality types that simply cannot work successfully together. It's not a failure; it's just how it is sometimes. If that's the situation in which you find yourself, it is time to seek alternatives.

What is the impact of the heart on the words we use? *Right speech* is a Buddhist concept that aligns compassion with the words we choose and the thoughts we think.

TRY THIS: RIGHT WORDS

Before you speak—before any words escape your mouth—ask yourself, are they kind? Are they necessary? Are they true? Begin with kindness and see where that leads. Helpful critique can be kind. How it will be heard is something to think about before offering it.

THE VOICE

In Chapter 1 we explored the impact of head-neck alignment and posture on how it makes you feel and how it impacts the way you're perceived. I touched a bit on how the voice is affected. Now moving on from the metaphorical aspects of "having" a heart, I'll take a deeper dive into the voice as it moves through the chest region. Indeed, it is impossible to discuss having an open heart without addressing the voice.

The voice mirrors and in many ways contains the life force. But almost no one—with the exception of actors, newscasters, preachers, and politicians—focuses on the voice with the proper attention. Defenses that seize the body can create tension in any number of places, but because the voice is such a profound manifestation of the entire instrument, it often manifests there. Take a moment to imagine any loved one and the way he or she sounds when excited, or sad, or suffering from an illness. Think of the sound of children when they play or are scared. Recall how, if you've ever read to a young child, you exaggerated the words, tune, and tone as a way of expressing emotion in the voice. Vocal signature is the manifestation of each person's unique style. Energy, strength, health, emotion, vitality—these are just a few of the things communicated by the sound of the voice.

Nasality, a flat droning monotone, filler sounds and words, vocal lift (that irritating habit of ending a statement with a questioning lifted pitch on the final words), poor enunciation, a too rapid pace, repeatedly dropping volume at the end of sentences—all these and many more unconscious vocal habits can totally misrepresent your knowledge, authority, and gravitas. Conversely, vocal mastery can greatly enhance presence, leadership, and the ability to connect. A voice should be easy to hear and understand as well as pleasant to listen to.

The voice is the result of torso and body shape and is affected by the breath, head-neck alignment, mouth, throat, jaw, and sinuses. Improper placement or chronic tension (due to defensiveness or for any other reason) anywhere along the route of voice production will impact how sound exits the body. Think of a cello; all of it is essential for the richness of tone, timbre, pitch, and volume. So in considering the voice, it is vital to understand the structure and connectedness of all aspects of vocal production, of the instrument that is your body.

An engaging, warm, lively voice is the result of linking feeling with intention via a relaxed body.

TRY THIS: TUNE IN

Turn on the radio, close your eyes, and really listen hard as you tune in to the announcer's pace, volume, tone, and pitch. Notice how a broadcaster will use variations of all of these elements to indicate what's most critical, the end of one segment, and the beginning of another. Focus on how he or she puts volume and emphasis on key words to indicate what should be noticed or remembered.

TRY THIS: STRESSFUL OR SOOTHING

Next time you're sitting on a park bench, at a cafe, or in a restaurant, close your eyes and notice the voices of those around you. Which ones make you feel agitated or stressed, and which calm you down? Do you see a pattern?

TRY THIS: WET DOG TALKING

Like a dog shaking off water, shake all over while speaking your name, address, and phone number or singing a simple tune like "Happy Birthday." Notice how the voice quivers and shakes as well. Why is that? It is *impossible to separate the voice from the body*, and it's essential that the body be as relaxed and centered as possible for the best vocal production.

Shallow-breathing, fast-talking, poorly enunciating speakers are difficult to follow not only in terms of the content they deliver, but more importantly because of the agitation and discomfort that they evoke in the bodies and minds of their audience. It is incredibly difficult to listen and absorb information when a speaker's delivery is choppy, monotone, littered with filler, or poorly enunciated.

Audiences want speakers to succeed. They worry when someone flounders while presenting. (When I say "audiences," I'm not only referring to large crowds. An audience is anyone on the receiving end of your communication.) But as much as audiences crave clarity of exchange and successful presentations, our pattern-seeking brains are instantly distracted and drawn in by a speaker's *flaws*. People have to work hard to tune out such things as filler words or vocal lift. That tuning out results in attention being divided and in reduced content retention. Pace will set off a response in an audience, too. If the pace is too fast, it will create a kind of agitation, and if too slow, it will lull people to sleep!

Susan Cain, the bestselling author of *Quiet*, has written about our work on her TED Talk. Tip #6 from "Seven Public Speaking Tips" (www.psychologytoday.com/blog/quiet-the-power-introverts/201109/seven -public-speaking-tips-coach-ted-speakers-and-ceos) is "If your voice is soft or high, try this exercise. Inhale. Open your mouth dentist-wide, and say ah in a low tone, holding your belly as if you expect it to vibrate (it won't.). Gina has to keep reminding me to keep my mouth wide open, because this feels so impolite to me. All of Gina's exercises feel impolite, come to think of it, which is no doubt why I'm sitting in her office in the first place."

I love Susan's remark about my exercises feeling "impolite," as so many things I ask of my clients force them out of their comfort zones. If you are an introvert, it will feel very strange to speak with greater volume; indeed beyond strange, it may even feel rude. Anything outside our usual range of motion, gesture, and volume may initially be experienced as "wrong." Once a habitually quiet person discovers a more robust, engaging voice, it is often supremely liberating. Beware those internal assessments (impolite, rude, wrong, unladylike, pushy, etc.) that hold you back from experimenting with different ways of experiencing your voice. Sometimes it is essential to push through the discomfort of a deeply ingrained limiter to find a new and more professionally aligned voice.

Problematic vocal patterns and voice production can also be the result of linguistic insecurity or emotional or psychological trauma. A British client—a lovely, fun, open woman working in Germany—received feedback that she was intimidating. I could not figure out why, as she was anything but. By sheer luck one day, I happened to be in her office when she answered the phone. No pleasant smiling "Hello," but a barking, harsh, very intimidating "*Yah!*" was her greeting. Bingo! Problem solved. Before her callers could even introduce themselves, her voice was telling them, "Be quick; I'm busy. You're interrupting me. Get to the point." German was not her first language, and by barking out her "Yah," she was unconsciously attempting to cover the concern she had regarding her language insecurity.

The voice contains one's history, culture, regional sound, psychological tics, and traps. It carries not only your tone but, more critically, your spirit and message. The physical sound of you exits your body and vibrates the eardrums of others, and what you say impacts their minds and hearts. Do you have a voice that speaks up, manifests your passion, courage, warmth, humor, and intelligence? Is there a disconnect between what you say and how it sounds? If so, that sets up an immediate, unconscious confusion in the mind of your audience. It is like static on the radio, and it's almost impossible to ignore. Vocal lift is a perfect example of this kind of split. This vocal-style pattern, making everything sound like a question, has become ubiquitous over the past few decades. It significantly derails a speaker's authority. In addition to being annoying, it's an unconscious "ask" instead of a confident "tell." When a declarative statement ends with vocal lift, it misrepresents the speaker and confuses the listener.

Tone is also a critical aspect of the voice. Tone is always aligned with intention or the goal of the communication. All communication is driven by moment-to-moment shifts in tone and intention.

TRY THIS: TONE TALK

Say "Sit down" as (a) a demand, (b) an invitation, (c) a plea, and (d) a question. Observe how the voice changes according to the intention behind those two simple words.

Entire books are available on the voice (see the list in Appendix C). But as far as "having a heart" is concerned, begin to observe your voice and ask yourself, "Is my delivery serving my role, my messages, and my heart?" It's vital to work consistently toward a vocal presentation that is fluid, alive, varied, and appropriate to the *goals of the exchange*. Ask yourself, "Is there warmth in my tone? Is there melody and pitch variation? Am I speaking at the proper pace for my audience? Do I leave room for silence? Am I too slow, too fast, using vocabulary that will make connections or be off-putting?" Keep in mind that brains seek the unexpected and pay more attention when it occurs. Variation of melody, pitch, tone, and pace will far more effectively engage your audience, while a monotonous, flat, repetitive style of delivery will surely impede connection.

TRY THIS: SUBTLE SUBTEXT

Take the sentence below and read it aloud, placing emphasis on the underlined word:

There is <u>nothing</u> in this store that I want to own.

There is nothing in <u>this</u> store that I want to own.

There is nothing in this store that <u>I</u> want to own.

Notice that by placing the emphasis on different words, the subtextual meaning and message of the sentence changes. Emphasis can be created by increasing the volume, by lifting or dropping the pitch on a word, or by pausing before or after a word. Observe the subtle changes in meaning that can be communicated. The exact same sentence can deliver widely varied subtextual intentions just by varying the emphasis placed on different words.

When writing a presentation or just speaking off the cuff, never underestimate the impact of vocabulary. One wrong word in a certain context can have significant ramifications not only on your message but on how you are perceived. I've witnessed entire negotiations fall apart due to a wrong word choice! I had a client who'd come to work in the United States from another country. He was creating a lot of problems by "ordering" his reports, saying, "You *will* do this; you *will* do that," or sometimes, just "Do it!" When I mentioned that kind of direct order can backfire depending on the recipient and that he might soften his approach with different individuals, he asked me what words to use. I suggested, "Let's," "How about," "Could we," "Have you thought about?" He barked at me, "But that is so *weak*!" He was unable to make the shift to a more inclusive vocabulary, and unfortunately he was let go. Tone has impact. Words have power. Choose yours with thought and consideration. Whether the goal is to connect, to lead, to inspire, or to enforce, it's imperative to have a rich, multilayered vocabulary that can work for the specific situation at hand.

The opposite spectrum concerns weak word choices. A client reported that she had an upcoming meeting where she'd have to present something about which she didn't feel 100 percent certain. "I'll be out over my skis" was her expression. "Off-balance. And I notice that in those circumstances I tend to use weaker verbs and less forceful language. I back off my own recommendations because I'm not quite certain of them. I use words like 'maybe,' 'could,' and 'I think' too much." Word choice is often a profound indicator of how grounded one feels. If uncertain about a subject, it is far better to lead with that truth than attempt to fake it with unconscious word choices that diminish your authority or send subtextual signals of insecurity. If you habitually use words that send those signals, even when you do feel secure regarding the subject matter, it is best to eliminate them from your vocabulary entirely. Practice saying the message out loud to find the words that support your message and do not undervalue it.

TRY THIS: SUBTLE TEXT

Write a directive, such as, "Finish the report, and have it disseminated by Friday at noon." Now rewrite it, considering how you might change certain words depending on your audience. Write it as it would go to your manager, your report, or a colleague. Pick a different colleague or report and rewrite it. Rewrite it as if it were going to a colleague in a foreign country. Were certain words more appropriate for a given audience or a given recipient's personality? Do you have a sufficiently robust vocabulary to make those subtle changes?

Now, take a more challenging communication and explore how, by varying the vocabulary, you might achieve different outcomes. Writing, as they say, is rewriting, and effective rewriting more often than not hinges on a solid grasp of the power of words: connotation, denotation, nuance, subtext, and cultural resonance.

We must constantly keep enriching our word choices and pushing ourselves to not rely on "packaged" phrases. As someone who spends a great deal of time hopping in and out of various corporations, it's fascinating to notice the "approved" cultural words that, like any meme, are said over and over and over again. These endlessly repeated words become trite, lifeless corp-speak, empty of meaning and devoid of power. It's essential for nuanced, audience-specific communications to embed novel words that capture the hearts and minds of your listeners.

One final word on vocabulary: different from filler sounds, like "um," but often serving the same purpose is "habit speech," words that are repeated unconsciously. "So," "I think," "Look," "You know," and "Like" are common. People have their unique repetitive verbal tics. Both filler and habit speech are ways that the mouth relies on sound to buy time while the brain is searching for a lost word or working to pull an idea together. The challenge with these unconscious sounds is that they can so litter the content that people begin to focus on them rather than on your ideas.

TRY THIS: HEAR YOURSELF

It's a good practice to occasionally record your voice so you can evaluate it objectively. People initially dislike the sound of their voice, as we all are accustomed to hearing it as it resonates within the bones of the skull. It sounds thinner and higher "outside" the head, but you can get used to it. Record your end of a phone call or long conversation and listen for filler words, habit speech, tone, and pitch variation. Ask friends and loved ones what about your voice is great or annoying, and pay attention to that part of you that, in some cases, is the only part others may *ever* know. Finally, make sure that your tone is aligned with your intention so that there is no confusion between the content and the goal of its expression.

If having recorded yourself, you notice a lot of filler sounds or words, the best way to limit or rid yourself of them entirely is to slow the pace of speech by just a tiny amount. Sometimes the mouth moves faster than the brain, or conversely the brain speeds ahead of the mouth. We reach an intersection where we need to either find the right word or catch our mouth up to our brain. We "fill" that moment of silence with sound. By slowing down the pace, we're better able to anticipate the intersection and often find the word when needed. The best way to slow our pace of speech is to enunciate more distinctly. It is hard to speak rapidly if the mouth fully wraps around all the sounds of a word, in particular, the end sounds.

TRY THIS: LAZY LIPS WORKOUT

If upon listening to your recorded voice, you notice that you mumble or have an abundance of filler sounds or repeated habit words, the best way to correct this is to slow the pace by enunciating more fully. Read aloud very slowly, enunciating in a very exaggerated way the beginning, middle, and end sounds of each word. Do this for one or two minutes a night, which is about all the lips and mouth will be able to tolerate. This is akin to weight lifting for the lips and mouth and is exhausting, but it works like magic! We all tend to have very lazy lips!

TRY THIS: FILLER BE GONE!

Say aloud your filler sound or habit speech very, *very* slowly. Repeat it 10 to 20 times to train both the brain to hear it and the body to feel the muscle recruitment that makes it happen. By repeating it extremely slowly and training the brain to hear it, you can stop it before it happens. Follow this by repeating just the muscle movements that precede the vocalization of the filler sound. Often, for example, "um" or "ah" is preceded by what's called a glottal stop. The base of the throat closes and obstructs the air flow. Feel that closing; repeat just that muscle movement over and over without making any sound. This will help the brain to notice just the movement, and then the filler sound can be replaced by a micro-inhalation. Do this in the morning after brushing your teeth. Repeat it daily for about 30 seconds over a week or two. By following this process, clients of mine have completely eliminated filler sounds. After you've gained mastery over this habit, repeat these exercises about twice a month, or the filler words will slowly creep back into your speech.

If, upon listening to your voice, you discover that your volume is either too soft or too loud, it would be good to ask others what their perceptions are. If they mirror your own thoughts, then you will want to adjust your volume. Additionally, I've found that for those who struggle with being heard or with getting traction from their comments, it can be something as simple as supporting the voice with a bit more power. The goal is not to feel as though you are pushing or yelling, but empowering the voice from the diaphragm. In the following section, I cover belly breathing, and following that is an exercise for increasing volume.

If you have any doubt regarding the power and influence of the voice, picture yourself sitting in a plane preparing for takeoff when the pilot makes the announcement. Imagine how you might feel if you were to hear a nervous, shaky, stammering pilot telling you to "sit back, relax, and have a nice trip." Could you? Would you? As seasoned and calm as passengers may appear, deep down they are giving up all control of their destiny for the next several hours. That's scary! Pilots know this. The only instrument a pilot has to send calm assurance to the passengers is that brief announcement. Calm, measured, warm—it's all been practiced so that the passengers relax.

One final thing to keep in mind: as our world becomes increasingly reliant on non–face-to-face communication, vocal mastery will only become more essential. Your voice is your signature. It's vital that it manifest your energy, warmth, smarts, and heart.

SHOULDERS

We've seen how head-neck thrust and poor posture can have significant impact on how you feel and are perceived. But what about just the shoulders themselves? Relaxed, upright shoulders with an open chest supported by a free open rib cage, all relying on the core strength of the abdomen, accomplish several things. One looks vigorous, open, robust, and able to take on challenges. Strong, relaxed shoulders and a lifted head greatly enhance a resonant open voice.

TRY THIS: FAN ARMS

Find a stool or chair without arms and sit in an upright position. Bend your arms and bring your elbows close in to the sides of your body. Notice the muscles between the shoulder blades, and *very* slightly engage those muscles. Float the head (imagine a string coming from the top of the head and going up to the sky, gently lifting you up. No yanking! No straining! Now, slowly, keeping the elbows by your sides, move the forearms outward to the sides (not forward) so that the forearms are perpendicular to the torso with the palms facing out. Then gently bring the forearms forward so that the palms are facing each other. Make sure the elbows stay tucked in next to your sides. Repeat five to seven times, making sure that the head stays lifted, is level, the chin doesn't jut forward, and the stomach muscles are engaged. This exercise utilizes the muscles in the upper back and counteracts the poor alignment resulting from hours at a computer. It's also excellent for opening the chest and shoulder area.

TRY THIS: THE BUTTERFLY

This exercise helps to open the shoulders and lead to a better head-neck alignment. Sit on the floor with your back against a wall and your legs extending straight out from your hips. Try to get your rear end as close against the wall as possible. Flex your feet by pointing your toes back toward your body; keep the legs straight and the thigh muscles engaged. The head should be touching the wall behind it and arms resting on the floor. As you sit in this position, gently bring the shoulder blades together. Hold this posture for two to three minutes.

TRY THIS: WEIGHTED NECK STRETCH

As you relax out of the butterfly position, keeping the chest lifted and open, drop the chin to the chest, bring your hands behind your head, and let the weight of the arms stretch the back of the neck. Take three or four deep belly breaths while holding that stretch.

When you consider the impact of posture on how you will be perceived, the reasons for good posture become immediately evident. Remember, the medium is the message, and when communicating, you are the medium. I had a client who had very slumped shoulders and such terrible head thrust that she required a thick pillow when lying on the floor. Her head simply could not reach the floor. After working to correct this situation, she called me to say, "I'm finding my voice!" I asked if she meant that her voice was more open and forceful. "Well, yes, that too. But I mean to say, I am speaking up! I realized that by being so slumped over, I was also not feeling the confidence to express my opinions. Now I am!" There's that body-mind loop again!

THE BREATH

Good posture is needed for proper breath support, which is essential for the voice. Although this chapter focuses on the chest region, we'll have to dive into the belly for a bit, as abdominal or belly breathing, the full expansion of the lungs that requires the belly to extend outward, is essential for proper voice production. Belly breathing is the restorative breathing we all do when we sleep and when we are relaxed. During the day, the breath immediately responds to any changes in circumstance. When nervous or stressed, we grip in the abdomen and take short, shallow inhalations into the chest. Often when I teach group seminars, I'll ask the participants to take a deep breath. Most of the people in the room breathe into their chests and not into their bellies. Shoulders go up, chests expand. Belly breathing, restorative, natural, deep, and essential for a calm, centered approach to all challenges, is often the exception rather than the rule. If you have children, watch them breathe in their sleep. You will witness their relaxed, round little bellies expand and then flatten, just as yours does when you sleep. Developing the ability to breathe deeply into the belly even when stressed or nervous is a skill that can and should be mastered.

TRY THIS: BELLY BREATH

Stand up, with the hips directly over the knees and knees over the ankles. The feet should be hip-width apart. Don't lock the knees; keep them soft. Float the head; again don't yank or pull it upward. Just imagine it floating upward in a gently lifted way. Keep the shoulders relaxed and down. Bring the shoulders high up the ears and drop them two or three times. Yawn once or twice. Now with the jaw relaxed, posture aligned, breathe in through the nose, and as you do so, let the belly expand fully outward. It can help to put one finger on your belly button, and as you inhale push the belly outward. As you exhale, let the belly button go backward toward the spine, or help that action by using your finger to gently push the belly button in. The chest and shoulders should not move at all. If you get dizzy, sit and continue, but make sure you are sitting up on the sits bones and not slouching. If you find this almost impossible to accomplish, then lie down on your back and read a book or magazine for a few minutes until you are completely relaxed. You'll notice that you are naturally breathing into the belly. Come to a sitting position and maintain that belly breathing. Stand and continue. If at any point when changing positions you find it difficult to maintain the belly breathing, return to lying down and start over. Be patient. For those who for decades have been chest breathing, this is a hard change to make. Keep at it, as the benefits—in stress reduction, energy, vocal power—can be huge.

Now that you've got belly breathing covered, below is an exercise that can gently and slowly build up the muscle to increase volume without yelling.

TRY THIS: CORNER SPEAK

Stand facing a corner with some reading material and read aloud at your typical volume for about a minute. Listen carefully so your ears and brain can assess the decibel level. Take one large step back and keep reading with the goal of achieving the previously heard decibel level. Read aloud for a minute. Do this for a few minutes each night for a week. On week two, repeat the above and step back two steps from the corner, again attempting to achieve the same decibel level, not by pushing or yelling, but by using the belly-breath support. On week three, repeat the above and step back three steps. Conversely, if you've been told that you speak too loudly, do the above exercise but in reverse. Start far away from the wall, attune your ears to hear the decibel level, and then step closer to the wall, lowering the volume accordingly.

Consciously working to slow down respiration when under duress has been shown to increase relaxation and tamp down the effects of adrenalin. The breath and heartbeat are instantly responsive to the sympathetic and parasympathetic impulses from the brain as it receives information from our surroundings. Developing mastery over the fight-or-flight effects on respiration is worth exploring, especially before a high-stakes presentation or communication.

TRY THIS: 10-SECOND BREATH

Relax the body and take a very slow five-second inhalation through the nose into the belly. If it is too hard to control the air coming in at that rate from the nose, then make a very slight opening in the lips. Exhale taking the same amount of time. Repeat six times. This can do much to help the body relax and focus, and it has been found to lower blood pressure and the levels of cortisol, the stress hormone.

TRY THIS: ABDOMEN VIBRATE

Relax the jaw and open the mouth very wide. Let the tongue come forward out of the mouth and stretch it gently forward. Now roll the tongue over the teeth as though cleaning them. Put one hand on the lower abdomen. Take a nice deep breath, keep the mouth open very wide, almost yawning-wide, and exhale on the sound of "hah." The mental exercise, along with this physical one, is to imagine the lower abdomen vibrating on that deep "hah" sound emanating from a wide-open relaxed jaw. It's very difficult to feel the hand vibrate while placed on the abdomen, but imagining it helps. Make sure you don't allow the jaw hinge to close down. Keep the mouth very open and head placed correctly on the neck. Make sure your head is level and not tilted up or down. Repeat 5 to 10 times. Don't think about volume, just vibration.

TRY THIS: CHEST VIBRATE

Continue the above and place your other hand on the chest. Repeat the relaxed, slow, deep belly-breath inhalation and now exhale on an "oh" sound. Don't reduce the opening of the jaw; keep the jaw wide open and create the "oh" sound with the lips alone. You will most definitely feel that sound vibrating in your chest.

TRY THIS: TORSO VIBRATE

With the jaw still wide and relaxed, keep the hands where they are and move the vibration from belly to chest. Switch between "hah" and "oh" sounds over multiple inhalations and exhalations. Try them on different pitch notes, moving up or down a scale from higher pitches to lower ones, or vice versa.

In addition to being very relaxing, these exercises open up belly and chest resonances for the voice. They are also excellent to do before any presentation, as they will get you breathing deeply, increase relaxation, and sharpen focus.

TRY THIS: BREATH WITH ARM THRUST

This breathing exercise can energize the body and is a way to release stress. Sit straight with elbows bent and hands beside the ears, palms facing outward. As you inhale, vigorously thrust the hands upward, palms open, fingers spread widely. As you exhale, equally vigorously bend the elbows and pull the arms back down to your sides with the elbows bent and the hands by the ears. Repeat this 5 to 10 times. It energizes and focuses the body. It's also a great practice for the mid-afternoon slump!

TRY THIS: GET THE PEANUT BUTTER OFF

Shake out all over, like a dog shaking water off its coat. Or you can do it in sections: raise the arms above the head and vigorously shake the hands, as though trying to get peanut butter off them. Bring the arms forward and shake the hands as if to say "go away" or "come back." Drop the arms to your sides and shake the hands up and down, up and down. No wimpy shaking; really move with energy! Add the hips: shake them side to side or back to front. Stand on one leg and shake the other as though trying to kick off your shoe. Switch feet. Finish by vigorously shaking your whole body. This is a great way to release tension and energize the body. I always add some deep grunting like a sumo wrestler for added fun and tension release.

ARMS/HANDS AND GESTURES

People often worry about what to do with their arms when they present in a more formal context. "What should I do with my hands?" is the most common question I get when I do presentation trainings. My first response is to tell my clients to replace the word *presentation* with *conversation*. The more you experience any exchange as a give-and-take, the better chance your hand and arm gestures will be an organic part of that exchange. Gestures and speech are deeply intertwined, so the best way to think about any content delivery, even a highly structured one, is for your style to be conversational.

Arms and hands are wonderful parts of our instrument and can greatly enhance the delivery of any message. They can also be terribly distracting. When we're tense, different tendencies appear: pounding the hands in rhythmic fashion, making chopping movements, conducting on the words, fidgeting fingers, rubbing fingers, gripping hands in front of the groin (known as the fig leaf position), keeping the arms frozen by the sides, hiding hands behind the back or in pockets. I've had many clients who were told early in their careers, "You use your hands too much," and they've spent decades with frozen, lifeless appendages ever since. Also, as with other aspects of communication, arm and hand gestures can be very culturally specific. "I'm Italian" is one explanation I've heard countless times from those who not only gesture vigorously but almost cannot speak without moving their hands and arms. On the other hand, a client from Pakistan told me that in Pakistan men stand with their arms crossed. This is their natural and comfortable position. He confided to me in a meeting, "Now that I'm working in the United States, I've been told that that is defensive and closed off, that I should have my arms open or by my sides. The problem is, if I do that, I literally lose my train of thought. I cannot find my words." Here is another stunning example of the body-mind feedback loop.

Language, speech, and gesture are all one connected system, not isolated parts. Studies have observed how infants' gestures and early speech are deeply entwined, as both are driven by communications needs. Babbling babies will often move their arms in sync with the sounds emerging from their mouths. As their gestures become more refined, and as pointing or raising their arms is used to indicate "pick me up," those gestures will then be accompanied by sounds. There is a mutual, flexible joining of gesture and speech that, once laid down, is almost impossible to decouple.

Whatever one's heritage and history, arm and hand gestures need to be genuine, relaxed, and appropriate. *They should align with your content and not compete with it.* Eyes automatically go toward motion and are immediately drawn to pounding hands and fidgeting fingers. It is best to eliminate distracting gestures and seek those that organically support the content. But also its important to avoid practiced, preplanned gestures, as they invariably come off as fake.

If you're really lost about how to let the arms express, the best choice is to bend your elbows and gently rest one hand into the other at midriff, not groin, level. That's a neutral and completely acceptable position. Once relaxed, arms move naturally. Between movements allow the arms to return to that hand-in-hand position, or let the arms relax by your sides. It's important that your hands are visible, so putting them behind the back is to be avoided. (Also, that position changes the shoulder line, thrusts the head forward, creating neck tension that can impact the voice.)

If your hands shake, a good technique is to use isometrics. By using the hand-resting-in-hand position, you can gently press the bottom hand up and the top hand down so that the shaking is diminished and that nervous energy is utilized by pressing the hands into each other. It should not be obvious and should appear relaxed. If you have a habit of putting your hands in your pockets, which is not recommended, try rehearsing while wearing pants without pockets. Explore where the hands can go without stuffing them out of sight.

Similar to recording the voice, the best way to see any distracting gestures and make the necessary changes is to videotape a rehearsal of you presenting. Seeing is believing, and by watching the recording, you can identify any habitual, repetitive, distracting gestures and work to reduce or eliminate them. A client with really large hands had a tendency to present with his hands held so high, they almost hid his face. I asked him, "Are you hiding your face or protecting it?" He had no idea to what I was referring until he saw himself on video.

"Hiding, no doubt," was his reply. "I've always felt a bit uncomfortable about my weak chin."

Some gestures are unconscious ways of hiding a part of ourselves, or used to distract the eye.

TRY THIS: HAND REST

To practice the best arm position for you, come to a standing position and let your arms go to your personal habitual position. Where do they go? Do you hold them behind your back? Put them in your pockets? To implement any change, it's best to become aware of your habitual hand or arm position. Relax and let your hands drop to your sides with your arms hanging loosely. Now bend at the elbows and gently place one hand into the other. Try not to interlace your fingers or press the fingers from one hand onto the fingers of the other (forming a triangle). The latter position, spider hands, can appear quite tense. One hand resting in the other is a great go-to position, as you can easily gesture from there and return to it with no effort.

TRY THIS: HAND DANCE

If you are really at a loss about what to do with your hands, it is best to get out of your comfort zone and do something wildly out of your usual patterns of movement. If you tend to stuff your hands in your pockets, force yourself to speak with your hands held above your head. If you tend to go immediately to the fig leaf position, put your hands on top of your head. If you feel you gesture too much, speak with your arms crossed. These are exercises to help you break habits and interrupt usual patterns of movement. The goal, obviously, is not to actually deliver with your hands above your head. It is to break the habit and see where the arms and hands go once the entrenched habits are broken.

TRY THIS: HAND WATCH

Since hand and arm movements are such vital parts of our overall communication, it's helpful to observe those who use gestures well. Watch closely those who use their hands effectively, who employ gestures that evoke the correct images, who use movements that lead the eyes and help tell the story. Additionally, since so many gestures are deeply embedded in culture, it is important, especially if you work in a global organization, to familiarize yourself with what may be unacceptable or rude hand gestures. Irrespective of culture, note as well those who use gestures that can be off-putting. Pounding, finger-pointing, fidgeting, tapping, unconscious repetitive rubbing—the list of what hands "tell" is remarkable, and it is wise to observe both effective and distracting gestures in others as a way of assessing your own.

A client who leads a team of over 30 people told me that he felt that many of them were not comfortable or open with him. As I listened to him, I felt myself feeling rushed and a bit anxious, and then I noticed his right thumb. His hands were folded on the table, but his thumb was constantly, and quite rapidly, beating up and down, sending a signal that my body read as "hurry up."

"What is up with your thumb?" I asked him. He had no idea what I was talking about. "It hasn't stopped moving since we began to talk. It's been wiggling up and down constantly."

"Really?" He took his hands off the table. Then, in an attempt to modify or control his wiggling fingers, he began to repeatedly run his hands through his hair. This was a replacement gesture and was equally disruptive. The source of his unconscious movements, what I call discharge movements, was energy bound up with tension. His body needed to move—a lot—but it had chosen repetitive, unconscious ways of doing so that created tension in *me*, and no doubt was doing so with his reports. As we began to unpack what may have contributed to the communication challenges at work, I decided to zero in on his thumbs. It proved to be the portal to a much deeper aspect of communication: how we mirror one another, which I'll explore more deeply shortly.

One final thought on hands as a part of our communication in the workplace: it is important not to underestimate the power of touch. Context is all with regard to touch, especially in the workplace, as it is a sensitive and tricky subject. Nonetheless, touch has been demonstrated to have enormous impact on connection. It is the primary form of exchange between infant and parent and is indeed its own language. (Soothing, comforting gestures can calm a baby who has not yet acquired any speech.) Touch is also very cultural, as some societies are far more open and comfortable with it than others. With regard to connection and its appropriate use in professional settings, it is always best to err on the side of less is more. Many employee handbooks simply state, "Do not touch. Ever." However, a firm handshake, a pat on a shoulder, a light touch on an arm, each of these can lead to a moment of exchange and trust. It's all in the timing, the duration, and the degree of eye contact. As far as having a heart is concerned, a gentle touch can work wonders. That said, a handshake that goes mere seconds too long, with overly penetrating eye contact, can suddenly shift from kind to creepy. But to simply never touch as a way to prevent potential infractions feels somehow inhuman. We are physical beings, and it is up to each person to create the boundary that establishes his or her level of comfort. More critically, it is essential that no one feel anxious or uncomfortable when either the giver or recipient of a touch. Hands are such a vital part of our overall communication that forbidding touch completely seems a deeply limiting response to a very human need.

MIRROR GAME/MIRROR NEURONS

Books on body language frequently explore how we unconsciously mirror one another's positions as a way to form connection and alignment. Some books even instruct readers on how to copy a counterpart's position or body language as a way to engender feelings of trust and rapport. Using an organic, unconscious system that evolved over hundreds of thousands of years for a multiplicity of reasons as a way to manipulate trust is, in my opinion, highly suspect. But exploring our desires to mirror and understanding our mirror neurons as a route toward compassion are extremely important.

In 1963, in *Improvisation for the Theater*, Viola Spolin introduced her theater games practices and philosophy to the theater community and, years later, into the educational and arts community at large. As time went by, her inspiring methods reached well beyond theater training and early education applications and entered the fields of psychology and mental health. Today, many team-building exercises employed by corporations and trainers have their roots in Spolin's games.

When I began studying acting at age nine, Spolin's games were the vocabulary of the day. Weekly, I would go to a two-hour acting class that routinely began with a warm-up called the Mirror Game. What was this exercise? In Spolin's words: "Player A faces Player B. A reflects all movements initiated by B, head to foot, including facial expressions. After a time, positions are reversed so that B reflects A."

Simple enough. As the players become more focused and adept, the game moves to a more complicated level. In Follow the Follower, the players "reflect each other without initiating. . . . Both are at once the Initiator and the Mirror. Players reflect themselves being reflected." The result is a level of riveting focus. The initiator-mirror relationship becomes indecipherable between the players.

There is neither leader nor follower. The players begin to experience the self not as "the" self but as "a" self, to step physically into another's reality of time, movement, intention, and sometimes even thought. It can be fabulously fun, sometimes a little scary, but no matter what, it's an enlightening experience.

My weekly practice of the Mirror gave me insight into other people that was beyond words. By mirroring an other I was wordlessly learning the power of entering someone elses' stance, expression, rhythm, indeed presence. As my skill improved, I experienced the awesome event when neither player initiated or copied, but when two distinct beings became synchronized. Talk about seeing things from the other's point of view! The mirror exercise, so simple, is utterly profound.

(Years later, when I was an acting teacher myself, one of my first classes was with teenagers from an inner-city high school. I was 19. They were 14 and 15. They were a tough bunch. Some had been expelled for knife fights or throwing chairs at their teachers. I taught them the mirror exercise and listened as they came up with every excuse in the world not to do it. But once they stopped giggling, settled down, and became focused, an amazing thing happened. They began to experience each other not as dangerous or alien but as fellow humans with whom they shared unspoken kinship. These were troubled kids, defensive to the hilt, but the game, once they got into it, opened them up tremendously. Wordlessly they dropped their habitual defenses as they embodied each other. They experienced stepping outside of themselves and into others' rhythms, movements, and expressions. They couldn't get enough of the mirror game.)

Spolin's exercise is a stepping-stone toward a critical skill everyone should aim to possess: become an other without judgment. The mirror exercise and, as neuroscience is discovering, our mirror neurons create the "merging of two discrete physiologies into a connected circuit."

While mirror neurons work at the unconscious level and the mirror exercise is done almost exclusively in acting classes, what can those who wish to consciously master the art of "merging discrete physiologies" do? After all, actors spend years mastering the art of signaling, spend weeks in rehearsal to make their characters come across as believable and authentic. How can those who've never studied such methods hope to achieve mastery over their communication skills?

The very first step is to bring awareness of your own body into consciousness. That, in itself, is a practice that must be integrated into daily life. Before you can consciously begin to understand the nuances of mirroring, it is essential that during the workday you check in, routinely and frequently, and observe your own body signals. Where is tension being held? What is your jaw doing? Your belly, your feet?

Our bodies communicate all day long, frequently expressing what we repress. Listening, checking in multiple times a day to the signals being sent *from oneself to oneself* is a critical first step. Awareness of your own physical state will provide deeper insight into the physical and emotional states of those around you. Self-scanning is the best first step toward this end.

When I first started to coach actors, while watching someone work, I'd occasionally get sleepy. Initially, I thought that I wasn't focusing well enough or that I was tired. But over time, I discovered that I tuned out or got sleepy when the performer was cut off, when he or she was just going through the motions, or phoning it in. The actor was *putting me to sleep*. Over time, I developed the skill of splitting my focus: watching an actor as acutely as possible while simultaneously listening to my body. If I got sleepy or restless or my mind wandered, it wasn't because I was undisciplined or tired. It was because the *person* was faking it, or hiding, or being some how inauthentic. If, while watching, my jaw got tight, my breathing shallow, or my back stiff, I began to realize that my body was at some level mirroring what the actor was expressing or, more critically, *repressing*. (There's actually a theater term called the *butt switch*. It refers to when the members of an audience as *a single body* unconsciously notice that their butts are falling asleep and need adjustment. When does this happen? Why would an entire group of people suddenly become aware of their discomfort? Because what is happening on stage isn't holding them. Because it's boring, ill-paced, or just plain bad. Even though an audience is made up of individuals, when they come together, they become akin to a giant brain, and they collectively know when what they are watching is not working. They may not have the vocabulary to say why, but they have the collective body smarts to feel it!)

So how might the mirror exercise be relevant to your workday? As humans, we are hardwired to observe each other in the most refined, minute, and instantaneous ways. In early human development, we needed to determine quickly if we were safe or in danger. Was the creature approaching out of the darkness coming to offer us something to eat or to eat us? Repeated miscalculations on instantaneous decisions of that sort would have had tragic consequences for the species itself! Additionally, for the survival of the tribe, we needed to instantly observe the bodies of those dependent on us. Was a baby crying because of hunger, sickness, discomfort, or boredom? Repeated incorrect interpretations of a baby's cry would have had terrible consequences as well. These ancient skills evolved for our very survival. We learned to sniff each other and our environments out instantly.

The theater is relevant because it is an outgrowth of those very same observational skills. And while these skills are indeed hardwired, they are subtle and require updating, fine tuning, and increasingly subtle awareness. The initial practice and ultimate refinement of developing one's own body awareness is a vital step toward understanding others.

TRY THIS: BODY SCAN

As you sit with this book in your hands, take a deep breath and mentally traverse your body by focusing your attention on your feet and then slowly moving that attention up your legs, knees, thighs, hips, groin, belly, chest, shoulders, neck, and head. Don't forget to notice your arms and hands. Where are you tense or tight? Are there zones or regions that feel deadened or, conversely, quite tingly and alive? Begin to practice this awareness randomly during the day, at your desk, while in meetings, or during conference calls. The routine of performing a mental checklist of the body is a profoundly enlightening exercise.

How to remind yourself to do this exercise? We have a multitude of technological devices—computers, tablets, cell phones—that can be set to vibrate, ding, or beep. Absent such things, there are Post-it notes or the age-old string around a finger. There will be resistance to "getting in touch" because we are so used to ignoring this thing we live in, taking it for granted until it tells us via injury, hunger, or illness to pay attention. The little voice inside rebels: "I have no time!" "I'm on the phone!" "I'm in a meeting" "I'm with a client!" But those are precisely the times to check in with what the body is doing and feeling. Body awareness can happen in the midst of any activity. All you have to do is shift your attention and check in. Initially you won't notice all that much. But the more frequently you do it, the better and more subtle your awareness will become.

TRY THIS: BAG OF SAND

Stop and take a slow breath; having located from the previous exercise where the tension is, attempt to release it. Focus your attention where you notice tension, take a slow inhalation, and imagine that there is a hole at the surface of the body where you feel the tension; then, like sand seeping out of a hole in a sack, imagine with each exhalation that the tension is seeping out through that imaginary hole. The more you develop this practice of becoming aware of tension and releasing it, the better you'll get at doing so. Ultimately, you'll be able to do this in mere seconds.

Once you are able to fully feel your body on a more consistent basis, to have greater awareness of the signals you are sending both to and from yourself, it becomes easier to be sensitive to those coming at you from others. You'll begin to notice when others are tense, when they are physically defensive, and when they appear to be listening but are in fact tuned out.

Occasionally, during communications trainings after a speaker has delivered a presentation, I will ask the audience if anyone's mind wandered. Initially, people are reluctant to admit that, while physically present, their minds went elsewhere. I only ask when it is acutely clear to me not that the audience was bored, tired, or indifferent, but that the speaker was not really engaged. Invariably 80 to 90 percent of the people in the audience will admit that their minds wandered. I'll ask, "Precisely when?" Again, invariably they will uniformly say, "Around slide three" or somewhere else quite specific. It is at that point that the speaker will then admit, "I didn't really want to deliver that slide. It bored me," or "I didn't fully agree with it." Mystery solved! The audience will tune out when you, the speaker, are not fully present or engaged. If you are bored by what you have to say, then how can you reasonably expect the audience not to be? Audiences know and feel this deeply, intuitively, and nonverbally. Developing the vocabulary to identify and define those behaviors within oneself only makes one more skilled at spotting them in others and becoming more adept at helping them. Additionally, I'll often ask a speaker if he or she noticed anything about the body at that particular point in the presentation. Invariably the response is a tightness in the throat or chest or restless legs. The body was expressing what was being avoided. Bodies talk reams, if we would only listen.

The take-away here is that by developing the practice of tuning in to your own body signals, you'll increase your skill at sensing those of others. By sensing others more acutely, allowing unconscious mirroring to become part of your communicative skill set, connecting with others will become easier and less constricted by judgment. On an even deeper and more consequential level, if your values are in conflict with something you must communicate, your body will at some level signal that, and others will at some level sense it. They may not be able to articulate it, but they will *sense* it.

The goal of an open heart, self-body awareness, and increased awareness of others—the mirror exercise, mirror neurons, neural Wi-Fi—goes beyond the ability to connect. It goes straight to the heart of being able to communicate with compassion. Why aim for this? Many reasons. Compassion, the ability to feel concern and care for another's difficulty with the accompanying desire to help, not only aids the sufferer but enhances one's own sense of purpose and engagement. By caring for oneself and others, we grow the muscle to better cope with distress overall. Perhaps this evolved over time as a way to ensure the survival of the species, but since we are all profoundly dependent on each other, it makes sense that concern for others' welfare would impact our own sense of purpose. Empathy, or the ability to feel emotionally what another is going through, while also vital for our common humanity, can overwhelm or lead to burnout. This is especially true for people who are constantly surrounded by those in distress. Compassion—the impulse to help, serve, and alleviate—on the other hand, tends less toward burnout and more toward engagement. What better way is there to connect and communicate effectively than through engagement?

The antenna deep inside all of us gathers signals from both ourselves and others, but it takes practice to tune in and develop it. Increased attunement leads us to make assessments and decisions in the gut before they happen in the brain, and that is where we'll go next.

Chapter 2: Have a Heart

Review Exercises

Heart

- **Embodied Aspiration**—increase confidence
- **Embodied Ick**—emotion-body feedback loop
- **The List of You**—identify old versus current self-labels
- **The List of Your Nemesis**—identify mirrors of your own negative traits
- **Open Heart**—release judgment, compassion
- **Right Words**—compassion

Voice and Speech

- **Tune In**—voice awareness
- **Stressful or Soothing**—voice impact
- **Wet Dog Talking**—voice-body connection

- **Tone Talk**—tone impact, tone control, tone choice
- **Subtle Subtext**—vocal emphasis, volume impact on meaning
- **Subtle Text**—audience awareness, vocabulary
- **Hear Yourself**—hear unconscious habits
- **Lazy Lips Workout**—enunciation
- **Filler Be Gone!**—reduce/eliminate "ums," "you knows"

Shoulders/Posture

- **Fan Arms**—back strength, posture, open chest
- **The Butterfly**—posture, alignment
- **Weighted Neck Stretch**—relaxation, stretch

Breathing

- **Belly Breath**—abdominal breathing
- **Corner Speak**—volume control
- **10-Second Breath**—relaxation, controlled breath
- **Abdomen Vibrate**—relaxation, vocal resonance
- **Chest Vibrate**—relaxation, vocal resonance
- **Torso Vibrate**—relaxation, vocal resonance
- **Breath with Arm Thrust**—energize, focus
- **Get the Peanut Butter Off**—energize, release stress

Arms

- **Hand Rest**—relaxed hand position
- **Hand Dance**—break habits, explore new hand and arm gestures
- **Hand Watch**—self-awareness

Mirror

- **Body Scan**—body tension
- **Bag of Sand**—relaxation

Exercise Name	Frequency Goal / Actual	Observations	Next Steps
Body Scan	Shoulders tense; do shoulder circles	Get tight belly before meetings with B.	Belly breath, choose point of view to calm me down, figure out why B. makes me nervous
	/		
	/		
	/		
	/		

Gut Smarts

*"It is through science that we prove,
but through intuition that we discover."*

—HENRI POINCARÉ

When I ask someone who is about to present where he or she feels the nervousness, almost invariably the person will answer, "In my gut." "Butterflies" is a common description of the fluttery sensation that shimmies around the abdomen. It can make one feel nauseous, tight, restless. The diaphragm tenses, preventing the lungs from expanding fully, and this results in short, choppy chest-breathing. Those symptoms can cascade from there to sweaty palms, shaky legs, light-headedness. In general, however, it all begins in the gut.

Gut instinct. Gut smarts. The gut knows, often before conscious realization, whether or not someone is trustworthy, whether a situation is safe or fraught with danger, and it tells us so with distinct sensations immediately. Add to this the concept of "having guts." To what does that refer? Is it to face danger with courage? To take risks that cannot be guaranteed successful? To speak up or, conversely, to remain silent? All of these can be true, and the person who "has guts" may exhibit them in one situation but be completely inhibited in another. Everything is situational. Irrespective of the circumstance and whether or not one takes action, the gut still knows. It tells us what we can and cannot tolerate. The question is, do we listen?

When I was an actress, I had a part-time job working for a small PR agent. By the end of my first day, I knew he was not a nice or honorable person, but I needed the work. I lasted with his firm for about three months, but it wasn't until I quit that I actually felt what my gut had been holding back. To this day, I can recall getting off the elevator and entering the office the morning after I'd quit. (I had to return for two days to finish out the week.) My stomach was no longer gripped with fear and tension. Indeed the stomachache, which I'd repressed for the previous three months, was gone. But what was shocking to me was that only by feeling its absence did I become aware of how unconsciously I'd buried my gut smarts the whole time I'd been employed by him. Unbeknown to myself, I'd tuned out my own chronic stomachache to survive within a toxic environment.

Gut sense, or intuition, can be defined as a combination of two kinds of intelligence: knowing, which is the result of expertise, and sensing, which derives from feeling. The first is characterized by a doctor who makes a diagnosis, seemingly from the gut, but in truth based on years of accumulated data and experience. The doctor has seen previous patients with the same symptoms, studied similar lab reports, and kept up on the most recent studies and research. The diagnosis is still in the "hunch" stage, but it is deeply informed. "Sensing" intuition is more like looking down a dark street late at night and thinking, "Nah, it looks a bit sketchy. I won't take the shortcut tonight." On what is that decision based? Sounds, darkness, the body sensing danger, which may or may not be there, but once the body is on alert, it's almost impossible to ignore. Historically, knowing and sensing were considered polar opposites, with the former considered the superior form of decision making as it was based on reason. More recently, they are being understood as parallel systems of decision making that work in tandem.

The gut is lightning fast, it's visceral, and it provides a snap judgment of a situation. It also tends toward hypothesis rather than certainty. The gut senses if an idea seems risky or ingenious, if a person seems genuine or phony. It's important here to distinguish between emotions and intuitions. Emotions are not intuitions, though strong emotions can often be confused with gut feelings. The difference is that emotions shift and change. You wake up in a bad mood, see your kid smile, and suddenly you're happy. Like candlelight, emotions flicker and shift with the breeze. But gut feelings stick. They are insistent. They won't let go. They ping over and over in the brain. They may not, in the end, be correct, but they cannot be ignored.

Where it gets tricky is that many of our gut instincts are the result of stored emotional memories from different life experiences. Early, preconscious events set up alarm systems that are unique to each individual's body. Conditioning begins as soon as we enter the world and continues throughout childhood. If you got food poisoning from a certain food when you were very young, chances are you'll avoid that food from then on. Even as an adult, it will be almost impossible to ignore the internal warning—*Danger! Danger!*—despite the knowledge that the poisoning was specific to one particular food item in one particular meal. This early warning system was designed for survival, and despite massive cognitive development over a lifetime of experience and learning, every new event is nonetheless measured against unconscious primary experiences. Additionally, our senses pick up cues before our thinking brain has the chance to analyze them. In milliseconds our instinctive, intuitive brain reacts, sending chemical signals to our body. So, for example, if a really big dog bit or even just snapped at you when you were two years old, chances are that as an adult, despite having had numerous encounters with nonaggressive dogs, your preconscious, instinctive reaction will nonetheless be one of fear. Conditioning, prior associations, traumatic events—these and more will color our gut reactions. Can we trust our gut that someone's not trustworthy merely because he *looks like* a dishonest coworker from our past? Of course not. But we do. Why? Because if there is something about a person, event, or situation that triggers that early warning system, the body reacts before we are even aware of it: the heart rate jumps; breathing shallows; palms sweat. The body alerts us, and suddenly, without consciously knowing why, we feel endangered. Ask yourself, what are some of your early life experiences that still trigger your gut? Are they still in line with what you know now? This is where the analytical mind needs to step in, observe the gut sense, and work with it. In other words, you can trust your gut but only to a point. The challenge is knowing *where to draw the line.*

It's essential to develop the self-understanding to question our own assumptions, to ask ourselves if our assessment is based in the reality of *this* moment or tied to a personal, historical association. The wiring for survival is smart and instantaneous but not particularly sophisticated. There was no time for sophisticated reasoning when a lion was attacking. But today, walking the corridors of the workplace, we're not being attacked by lions (although that depends on where we work). Nonetheless, the fight-or-flight system can't make the distinction between a literal lion, a metaphoric one, or even a loud noise. For our reactions to be most effective, we need to be able to differentiate emotions from gut intuitions. This is where I recommend checking back in with the body itself. If the belly tightens, there is valuable information being sent to the mind, but is it reliable? That tight belly may be indicative of antiquated, conditioned responses that are no longer in concert with the present. Or it may indeed be a valuable signal that needs to be attended. If the belly feels loose, happy, and eager, that too is valuable information. The dialogue *between* body and thought requires our attention and asks each of us to develop a refined language of description, definition, and awareness.

A common challenge is chronic, gut-churning distress when there is discord between one's personal values and the values of the workplace. Often this can be further compounded by a contradiction between the stated values of the organization and the actual behaviors that are tolerated. An organization may say that it values people who speak up but, in fact, punishes or demoralizes those who do. For those who are expected to present a lot within such a contradictory culture, it is extremely taxing. Why? These are crazy-making situations, which go right to the gut. When misalignment or mixed messages collide with one's personal values, the result is a sense of being off-balance. To stay employed, one may be compelled to bury one's true self and manifest an expected persona. This conflict can impact the body in multiple ways, but most often, it's experienced as tight, churning tension in the gut. To persist in such an environment, that tension must be endured or suppressed and can become so habitual that it's no longer even sensed. (This is what my body did when I worked for the PR firm.) The tension resides inside the body as a dormant volcano, unpredictable and potentially quite disabling.

When threatened, we tend to clench the abdominal muscles to protect ourselves from assault. This is similar to the cowering of shoulders and neck mentioned earlier in the book. Given the endless, albeit nonthreatening, daily stresses that many currently endure, chronically tight bellies are to be expected. (When I say "nonthreatening," I mean non–*life* threatening.) The fight-or-flight response in primordial times was triggered perhaps once every few days; now it is set off multiple times *every day*. When a booming jackhammer pounds through the day, we do everything possible to tune it out. But if we suppress the inner tightness of a chronically stress-triggered gut, we cut off the intuiting brilliance that resides there. Additionally, by living with constant stress and repressing our gut smarts to do so, we exhaust ourselves. This is not the exhaustion that's the result of hard work; it is the exhaustion that comes from being in a state of conflict with oneself. Result? Alive but not vital! Here but not present. At work but not engaged. The energy that could be expended in so many creative and productive ways is directed to appease the war within. End result? Armies of the emotionally cutoff undead (and my personal theory about why zombie games and movies are so popular!). The smart gut evolved to protect us from danger. But overscheduled lives, tension, and chronic stress cut us off from our very own internal genius. All these factors profoundly influence our communication and impact our ability to effectively be in and manage the present moment.

All professionals spend years mastering their craft until it becomes intuitive. It seems ironic, but the goal is to so deeply integrate those skills that they become second nature and the pro can then be in the moment and go with his or her gut. In the theater, a consistent performance needs to be delivered night after night, but every actor knows that Saturday night's audience will not be the same as Friday's. How can a performance be consistent when every night and every audience is unique? The attuned actor adjusts moment by moment to the subtle audience shifts. When an audience laughs, the attuned actor senses when the laughter is peaking, holding off delivery of the next line for just the right amount of time to let the laugh finish but not die out completely. Some actors seem born with these intuitive skills, while others must train to attain them. But they are teachable.

In any professional communication, the audience—be it colleague, manager, or client—is as alive, unpredictable, and changing moment by moment as you are. To connect, in a discussion, a formal presentation, a group meeting, or a negotiation, it's essential to pay acute attention to all the minute, rapidly shifting signals speeding by. Consider any business encounter as the actor does the audience. Why? Because life is essentially a never-ending, unpredictable improvisation. If you've gained the skills and expertise to navigate the unexpected, your gut will guide you on how to do so. But if for any number of reasons you've cut off your own belly smarts, that organic creative flow will be blocked, and what you'll be left with are missed signals, ignored cues, lost opportunities.

Tension, whether chronic or due to sudden unexpected stress, removes us from the moment, cuts us off from our own self-awareness. If we refuse to let go of a predetermined idea of how an encounter should unfold, and it doesn't, what happens? We are at loggerheads with the present. That conflict manifests as pushing without listening, arguing without honoring, judging without respecting. How often, watching people present, have you observed them cut off a questioner, interrupt a speaker due to refusing to let go of predetermined outcomes? Where does such behavior come from? What triggers it? Is its source physical, emotional, or psychological?

Tension is the result of an infinite number of influences, but one of its greatest triggers is time. We have an ancient, hardwired hormonal clock that is now in continual battle with the modern world. To assess our ability to accomplish all that we ask of ourselves, to understand how we experience time, we need to listen to our *body clock*. It is there, ticking away, sending vital, intuitive knowledge about how much we can handle and when to handle it. Chronic time stress affects our normal circadian rhythm. Small, occasional doses of stress hormones have been shown to be somewhat beneficial to thinking and performance. But endlessly high levels of adrenaline and cortisol can affect everything from weight gain to bone density. The gut knows what it can and cannot tolerate and for how long.

What do you do on a daily basis that pushes you beyond what your body naturally wants, needs, and tolerates? How does that impact your daily communication, and how you deliver information, how you listen? What body signals do you ignore due to your sense of time and busyness? Do you jam too much into an exchange or presentation? Do you speak at a pace that loses people? Do you interrupt people? Do you cut off speakers during meetings? Do you fidget while listening or speaking? How do these behaviors go beyond yourself and impact how you connect with those around you?

We need to relax into our bellies, and to do so often. By tuning in to habitual defense mechanisms, chronic stressors, and subconscious triggers, we can navigate the present moment far better. We need to remind ourselves to give up our "imagined" results of how an encounter, presentation, or communication should go and work to connect with this moment *as it is*. Quite literally, we need to breathe *into* the moment, not harden against it. Only then can we hope to find alignment when communicating. Alignment, by the way, is not necessarily agreement. We can disagree. It's OK to have different opinions. They're actually very important, as they enable learning and growth. But when we perceive disagreement as threat, we tighten the belly, withdraw, defend, or shut down. Letting go of belly tension is an amazing way to stop habitual patterns and to get back to finding points of connection.

TRY THIS: SOFT BELLY

This wonderful exercise allows one to let go of tension in the gut and, with practice, to flood oneself and others with compassion. It seems crazy, but it's true. As you sit reading right now, let *all* the muscles in your abdomen completely relax; let them just melt into a loose puddle of softness. Don't worry if you look fat! Close your eyes, take a deep breath, and simply let *all* the belly-holding go. The belly may attempt to grip. Don't let it. Let it go and stay with it for a few breaths. Just experience how, by completely softening the belly, the feelings and emotions begin to bubble up. In general, the most profound emotion that comes to the surface is tenderness, a soft forgiving acceptance.

"Soft Belly" does not have to be done while you are alone. It is good to do during any high-stakes communication, stressful meeting, or negotiation. It does not make you weak. It makes you open, to yourself and your counterpart. As you encounter conflict with someone at work, instead of tightening the gut, train yourself to do the opposite. Let the belly go completely and experience what happens. It is counterintuitive, as it conflicts with the survival mechanism to tighten; but remember, a squabble with a colleague is not a lion attack. The ancient brain doesn't know the difference, but a conscious self must learn to distinguish. "Soft Belly" practiced in the midst of a disagreement has the potential to quickly shift the dynamic from aggressive and defensive to calm and open.

During a formal presentation with interactive questions, the use of "Soft Belly" is an excellent way to defuse tension, to encourage better listening and less defensive answers to questions. Managing butterflies, a gripped gut, even nausea, when nervous about delivering a presentation, is a skill that can be learned. The techniques to do so must be practiced and embedded long before the event itself, so that they become routine. The best practices to counteract nerves are "Belly Breath," "10-Second Breath," and "Wet Dog Talking" (see Chapter 2). These, in combination with the tips listed below, can be tremendously effective in dealing with presentation nervousness that grips the gut.

By practicing both "Soft Belly" (above) and "Open Heart" (Chapter 2), you will experience subtle but quite distinct differences. Releasing and opening in each center creates different emotional responses. By frequently practicing one, or both, especially in the midst of stressful business communications, your body and thoughts will begin to respond in novel ways. By shifting focus from the subject at hand, the body instinctively takes a deep, cleansing breath. That breath acts as a needed pause, an interruption. It provides space for new thoughts and different, less habitual, responses.

TRY THIS: BELLY IMAGINE

Close your eyes and picture someone you would love to see—a beloved relative, an old friend—and imagine him or her sitting a few feet in front of you. Now go into your belly area with your mind's eye and see what it feels like.

Now try it with someone you dislike and never wish to encounter. Put him or her a few feet in front of you and again feel what the belly says. The feeling may be subtle or acute; the goal is to be aware, pay deeper attention, and begin to notice what the gut says.

TRY THIS: BELLY FEEL

Think about an idea that you have for an exciting project at work. It may not even be part of your job description. Whatever it is, it should be something exciting that you look forward to accomplishing. Really imagine how you might fulfill this idea. If it's a solution to a problem, imagine all the steps you might take. Jot them down. After a few moments, check in with your belly and see what it feels like.

Along with practicing "Soft Belly," another excellent practice is to check in with the entire body at random times of the day for 10 to 15 seconds. This is slightly different from the body inventory of tension mentioned in the previous chapter, as it has different results.

TRY THIS: TUNING IN TO THE TUNED OUT

Try to consciously feel what the brain tunes out: How do your feet feel in their shoes, your belt around your waist, the rings on your fingers? Our brain tunes out these constant physical sensations; otherwise it would be flooded with unnecessary information. *Habituation* is the term for this tuning out, but one problem is that we tune out so much else. The classic "Stop and smell the roses" I've modified to "Stop and sense the habituated." (It doesn't have quite the same ring to it, but you get the idea.) Can you sense your tongue in your mouth? Feel your heart beat? Become aware of blinking? Feel your kneecaps, your rear end? Can you go deeper and feel where there is joy or sadness or fear inside the body? How the self experiences emotions through the senses? How it sends those emotions through the body? Now focus specifically on your belly and determine what feelings are predominant in the center of your being.

Why do this? "Mindfulness meditation," mental focus for 10 to 20 minutes a day on the breath or a mantra, repeatedly recommended by everyone from ordinary schoolteachers to gurus, is an almost impossible ask. Despite all the research on its benefits, most people simply cannot (or more likely, will not) find the time. Many don't have the discipline to follow daily meditation practice. But the good news is that even brief targeted attempts at awareness done throughout the day can have profoundly beneficial effects. Aim for 5 to 10 mini-meditations of 30 seconds to a minute and a few breaths. Tune in to any of the habitually tuned-out areas of the body or just to the belly. Clients to whom I have recommended these exercises have reported many surprising and wonderful results. Below is one of my favorite e-mails from a client:

"It sounded crazy to me, but I began to try 'soft belly' in my weekly departmental meetings. It became clear almost immediately how much more patient I felt. Time didn't feel so crunchy. So I taught it to my team. They thought I was crazy. But now, when things get tense, I'll call a 'time out for soft belly,' and we give ourselves fifteen seconds of cooling off. Sometimes we just wind up laughing. If nothing else it's been a great stress-buster. THANKS!!"

We do not yet understand fully all the systems that make the intuitive belly so smart. Biochemical, neurological, electrical, and even microbial influences are all contributors. (Yes, increasingly, we are learning that microbes may in fact be running the show!) Whatever makes the show go on, the gut knows a lot, and we would do well to take the time and deep breaths needed to listen.

Chapter 3: Gut Smarts

Review Exercises

Abdomen

- **Soft Belly**—relaxation, compassion
- **Belly Imagine**—emotion-body feedback loop
- **Belly Feel**—emotion-body feedback loop
- **Tuning In to the Tuned Out**—body awareness, relaxation, focus

Exercise Name	Frequency Goal / Actual	Observations	Next Steps
Soft Belly	Before and during conflicts with colleagues	Was able to listen better, reduced defensiveness	Do even when not in conflict to see how that impacts my listening skills
	/		
	/		
	/		
	/		
	/		

Exercise Name	Frequency Goal / Actual	Observations	Next Steps
	/		
	/		
	/		
	/		
	/		
	/		

Standing Tall

*"It is absurd to divide people into good and bad.
People are either charming or tedious."*
—OSCAR WILDE

HIPS, LEGS, AND FEET

We so rarely think about how we move in space and time. But movement, similar to posture, facial expressivity, and all the other ways we inhabit our body, has a huge impact on how we feel and the influence we have on others. Your walk is as much your signature as your voice is. Hips, legs, and feet—the bottom half of us—rarely get the kind of attention that we give our faces, hair, and hands. They should, as they significantly affect how we are perceived.

A client was sent to me to increase her executive presence because she was being considered for a promotion, but there was something stiff and rigid about her style. She was smart but lacked warmth. Her movements were sharp and fast-paced. She was an avid runner and quite thin. At work, she didn't walk; she *flew*. Those who knew her well accepted her pace. But people unfamiliar with her rapid pace would think, what's the crisis? She appeared out of control, even though that was not the case. But her too rapid pace set off alarms in others. As someone being considered to be head of communications for a multimedia conglomerate—itself often in the news—her style needed to shift. She was in front of the media and senior management, presenting constantly. We worked long and hard on modifying how she moved. We slowed down her walk, relaxed her stride. This was hard and took a lot of time, work, practice, and concentration on her part, but the change was remarkable. *By just slowing her pace, she was able to shift how she was perceived.* Equally important, slowing down enabled *her* to perceive things differently. It's akin to what you can absorb when driving at 30 miles per hour versus 70. The details that one loses when in a state of hyperspeed suddenly come into focus and can be analyzed and appreciated quite differently. The change in her pace also had a huge impact on her sense of calm and control. Her newfound ownership of time did not end with her body alone. Calmness, like a breeze, can flow across a room and ease the stress and anxiety of others. (Recall how pilots use just their voices to calm those aboard planes, as mentioned in Chapter 2.) As she relaxed, those around her relaxed, too. She was not known for being a particularly warm person, but as she slowed down her walk, her style began to shift and soften.

Every workplace has its unique culture, and I can quickly tell if an organization is lively, inventive, and welcoming by something as basic as how people walk and move. Do I hear laughter? Are people casually chatting? Do people make eye contact and smile when they see each other? Do they walk down hallways in ways that are comfortable and relaxed? Is there an office energy? Or is the environment airless and shut down? (Once, when interviewing for a certain firm, I was told, "We are a slate gray and navy blue company. No pink skirts or shoes here." Needless to say, I didn't pursue the opportunity. On the other hand, I was grateful the company was so clear about its style.)

In the work environment, what is the proper balance between exhibiting one's own sexual energy and life force and slipping too far, bordering on the inappropriate? Obviously, men and women bring different energies, styles, and approaches to all sorts of challenges, and those differences should be welcomed and explored by all organizations. By repressing our life force and gender orientation, we disable powerful forces of creativity and problem solving. Hips, legs, feet, and walks are a good place to explore the degree to which an organization is rigid, overstressed, or relaxed.

As a casual observer, I've noticed that one of the deals we've made for the workplace to be safe is for it to be sexless. I'm in no way suggesting that workplaces should be full of romping, sexed-up employees! The office is not the place for that. What I am suggesting is that people not become wooden, cutoff, asexual drones forbidden from expressing the vital energy that is at the core of our very existence. One thing that strikes me at many organizations is how much overt sexism is present and how much sexuality is absent. (I have observed the most blatantly sexist, demeaning signage in a women's restroom, literally instructing them on how to wipe and flush. At the same organization, I asked some men if there were any instructions in their restroom. I received a blank stare, followed by, "What the heck are you talking about?")

The core, as I see it, is a behavioral defeminization many women attempt in order to be taken seriously by men and an excessively remote style affected by men to avoid being perceived as sexual predators. This directly affects the impact of communication. Libido, or life force, is powerful stuff, which puts us in touch with different points of view. By not repressing it, we allow for a far more inclusive, creative environment.

How to bring that life force at the core of one's gender into the workplace or into a presentation without it becoming a derailer—or having the PC police called in? Simple. Instead of gender, think charm; instead of flirting, think warmth. Charm, warmth, openness—these are assets belonging to *all* of us *irrespective* of gender. When, in order to be taken seriously, we cut off our life force, dampen down our joy and sense of fun, we also suppress some of our greatest gifts. Being warm does not mean being weak. Women and men confuse and limit themselves when deciding that softer, more "feminine" modes of expression make them vulnerable or weak. Similarly, a "hard" affect, with its attendant lack of charm, limits and cuts off the very qualities that are delightful and engaging. Think about your own work relationships. With whom would you rather work, someone who is open, warm, fun, and engaging or someone who is tight, cut off, and demanding? What happens inside your body—observe those microfeelings and signals you experience—when heading into a meeting with someone warm and open versus cold, bossy, and humorless? Remember, everything is situational. Certain communications and circumstances require a harder affect. What matters is that your ability to manifest warmth and charm is not extinguished due to the culture of your organization.

TRY THIS: BEACH WALK

Do this at home. Close your eyes. Imagine you are at the beach. Hear the surf; feel the sand between your toes and the sun on your skin. Now, open your eyes, keeping them down, and slowly walk around your yard or home with that mental imagine. Notice your pace and how the hips and legs move. What happens?

TRY THIS: OFFICE WALK

Do this at home, too. Now mentally put yourself at the office. Do your office walk. What does that feel like?

We cannot, and should not, walk at the office in the same manner as we do when at the beach. Such a slow, languorous style would be situationally inappropriate. Nonetheless, the impact on the hips and their range of motion when we're tense and walking stiffly can be significant. Is there a way to find a blend between the two?

Think back to adolescence and try to recall how and when you grew. It's fascinating how growth spurts that happen between our preadolescence, puberty, and mid-teens can impact one's habits and gestures throughout life. A female client, over six feet tall, grew almost a foot taller than all her classmates in junior high. She tried to make herself shorter by habitually crunching her lower abdomen and hips and bending her knees. In attempting to hide her height, she actually drew attention to it. On the other end of the spectrum, a male client, who never reached the height he'd aspired to, constantly went up on his toes when presenting. Both of these distracting compensations began when they were adolescents and remained well into their professional lives.

When I observe deeply ingrained compensatory movements and gestures, I often ask the client to describe what he or she recalls from growth during puberty. Not always, but often, there is something about how the body changed during that critical time that made the client attempt to hide or compensate for that change. That period of life is rife with self-consciousness. Eventually we grow up and learn to live with and perhaps even enjoy the new body we occupy. But if a gestural, postural, compensatory habit begun around puberty becomes integrated into the deep layers of muscle memory or movement, it can remain part of one's signature style of movement from then on. Creating the link to the memory is the first step. Practicing new, more aligned habits of movement is the next. Finally, I encourage my clients not just to accept their body as it is, but to *own* it. *Own* your full height if, in your 13-year-old mind, you are still too tall. *Own* your size if, in your 16-year-old mind, you are too fat. Awareness of the habit, integrating new ways of moving to break the habit, and ultimately embracing new ways of conceptualizing the body is a liberating process.

So much is communicated by how we move, and often that movement is restricted by the pelvic girdle in the hip area. The pelvic girdle is the linchpin of our posture, as it unites the upper and lower halves of our body. The lower half is designed for motion: running, walking, climbing, kicking; the upper half for throwing, grabbing, carrying, hugging. The hip and pelvis region functions as both a hinge and a fulcrum, allowing the spine to be flat or bent and, when necessary, to be quickly hoisted upward. Unfortunately for many, the pelvic and hip region moves in a dysfunctional way. The most common manifestation of this movement is a lumbar arch in flexion. The lower spine has a lovely arch that curves slightly forward, toward the belly. But when the lumbar arch is in flexion, usually from years of sitting improperly with the mid-body collapsed, many suffer from an arch that's curved outward. The result manifests throughout the rest of the body in many, often troubling, ways.

TRY THIS: SEATED PELVIC TILT

As you sit with feet flat and about 10–12 inches apart, knees at right angles, gently bend at the waist and slowly roll the pelvis backward so that the lower back curves toward the back of the chair. Now roll the pelvis forward so that the lower abdomen comes forward and the arch in the lumbar, or lower back, region is exaggerated. Roll backward and forward slowly, feeling the lower back move through those two extremes. Find the midpoint, where the back has a slight curve forward and the weight is evenly distributed on the two sits bones at the base of the hips. How does this compare with your usual posture while seated?

TRY THIS: BELLY DANCE

Come to a standing position and bend your knees slightly. Bend forward and place your hands on your knees. Curl the lower back by bringing the lower abdomen toward the floor, which will arch the lower spine; then reverse the curl, bringing the lower abdomen upward and moving the lower back into flexion toward the ceiling. Repeat this 10 to 15 times. This is also a great way to warm up the lower back and bring circulation to that region of the body. Remove the hands from the knees and stand straight. Now add side-to-side movements, swaying the hips from right to left. Finish with full hip circles, moving the hips in large, wide circles starting on the right side, moving forward, then to the left, then back, and to the right. Do three or four circles in that direction, and then go the other way.

TRY THIS: OPEN HIPS

After completing a few hip circles, grab hold of a chair or something comparable for balance. Bend the right knee, open the knee out to the right side, and circle the leg a bit behind you and then bring it forward. Rest the right foot on the floor and then repeat the motion. Do five or six knee circles with the right leg and then five or six with the left. This rotation helps to loosen up the hips and pelvis.

TRY THIS: TAKE A THOUGHT FOR A DANCE

Before a high-stress presentation, combine the point-of-view exercise "Take a Thought for a Walk," described in Chapter 1, with movement. Put on some earphones, play your favorite upbeat song, think the thought, or point of view, and let yourself dance to the music. Listening to music is a great way to shift point of view and evoke different emotions. Since we often associate memories with music, it's good to create your own go-to playlist for different situations. Just listening and dancing along to a few bars can work wonders for your state of mind.

When seated at your next meeting, pay close attention to where your hips and pelvis are positioned. Many people tend to put the bulk of their weight on the mid- and upper rear end, leaving a large space between the lower back and the chair. This is fine as an occasional go-to position, but not a position in which to remain hour after hour after hour. It puts a lot of strain on the lower back and creates a collapsed middle. As much as possible, attempt to sit on the sits bones, with your arms resting on the table, not your lap. This position allows you to turn your upper torso quickly to face someone on either side of you. It communicates energy and looks more engaging.

● ● ● ● ●

With the exception of buying shoes—or wearing ones that hurt!—hardly any people think about their feet. But we should. Feet are our connection to the earth, our movable roots. They greatly influence our pace, our sense of being grounded, and our ability to stand firm and tall. Feet also express feelings. Happy babies frequently express those emotions by vigorously wiggling their legs and feet. Adults, when impatient or in a hurry, will often tap their feet or unconsciously shake their legs and feet. When presenters are nervous, one tendency is to shift the weight from foot to foot or take small steps backward and forward. One client, when presenting a new idea, literally took a step back with each new slide. By the time he got to his sixth slide, he was almost against the rear wall of the room. It was as though his feet were backing him away from his very own suggestions. There's subtext again!

TRY THIS: FEELING FEET

As you sit, wiggle your feet as though you are excited. Now tap your feet, as if in a hurry or impatient. Now, keeping your toes on the floor, quickly lift the heels up and down, shaking the legs as a result. What does each of these foot movements make you feel?

Feet are amazingly structured and incredibly complex. The arch of the foot (there are actually three, but most know only the large one at mid-foot) must support weight and provide stability, while the joints, muscles, and bones must be flexible and adapt to changing surfaces. Propulsion, bearing weight, and balancing are the three critical functions of the feet. To be centered before delivering a communication, whether seated or standing, proper use of the feet is essential.

TRY THIS: CENTERING

To use the feet effectively, your weight should be distributed evenly and the toes engaged. Stand, making sure your knees are aligned over the ankles and not locked, your hips are over the knees, and your legs are hip-width apart. Your ribs should feel lifted off the hips, not thrust forward. Imagine your head floating. Shift your weight slightly from your heels to the balls of your feet a few times and then find center—where the weight is distributed evenly between the heels and the balls. This stance is both powerful and grounded, as well as instantly flexible and ready for action. Now press your toes into the floor as though they are grabbing a tree limb. You will feel the quad muscles in your thighs engage and your body shift slightly forward of the center of gravity. The bottom half of your body will root itself like a tree trunk.

TRY THIS: LAUNCH

Become centered as described above, press the toes into the floor, take a deep breath, and smile. This is charm rooted in strength and warmth with stability. Now take that feeling on a walk. Walk around your living room and see how it feels to launch your gait from a grounded stable position.

TRY THIS: LONG STEP/SHORT STEP

Take a walk and expand your gait by just a few inches. What does that feel like? How does that impact your walk and sense of self? Now do the opposite. Shorten your gait by just a couple of inches. What does that feel like? Now speed up that shortened gait. What message might that send to those around you? Now slow it down. Explore varied paces and lengths of gait to see how they make you feel and also what they signal outward.

I recall reading about a study years ago in which muggers were asked to watch videos of different people walking and identify whom, based on their walk, they would mug. It turned out that instinctively they chose people whose gaits were either too short or too long for their heights, thus making them slightly off balance and easier to destabilize.

For presentational situations that are more formal, keep in mind that you are on stage from the moment you leave your seat. If there is a rather long distance from your seat to the stage, make sure that your walk, pace, and posture are in a style that best signals your presence.

Consider your walk as your metaphor. I had a client who was a "stomper." Her heels hit the floor with such force when she walked that she could be heard approaching several moments before her actual arrival. Her colleagues and reports would tense up at the sound of her approach. Her walk was also a physical manifestation of how hard she stomped on herself. A perfectionist, she was very demanding of herself and others. While we worked to adjust and soften her style, I didn't ask her to tiptoe, but I did suggest she try to walk without making such a racket. I hoped that by softening her inner critic along with her outer movements, the two, in tandem, might allow her to ease up on herself, while also letting her be perceived more positively by her colleagues. She was delighted to report that once she'd quieted her walk, those who'd formerly tensed up at her approach confessed that just hearing her coming always made them anxious. Even more exciting, stepping lightly became a reminder not to be so hard on herself.

Another client was great one-on-one but felt shy in groups, finding it difficult to contribute. He'd see a small group of coworkers chatting and want to join in but had trouble entering an ongoing conversation. I suggested he try the toe exercise ("Centering") mentioned above, to stand tall, gently press his toes into the floor, and feel his legs become a great tree trunk of support. I asked him to imagine that he was not joining or jumping into a conversation, but warmly inviting the coworkers *into his*, playing the host. The mental shift, along with the slight adjustment and awareness of his toes, gave him the confidence to get out of his head and into the conversation. He reported back that he'd had no idea that toes could be such a powerful influence on confidence.

This feeling can be evoked also while seated.

TRY THIS: SITTING TALL

It's very simple. Rather than slouching, allow the back to be straight and the sits bones at the base of the hips to support the body. Bend the knees at 90 degrees, place the feet flat on the floor, and press the toes gently into the floor. Place arms on the table without collapsing and without putting a lot of weight or leaning on the arms. Just let them rest comfortably.

TRY THIS: WALK COPY (Part One)

When you head home from work today and are walking from your office to your car, bus, or train, pick someone about 10 feet ahead of you and copy that person's walk. I can imagine the resistance: "What if someone sees me?" "That's weird!" "Why would I?" First off, no one is watching, and strangers don't know *your* particular walk. Why do this? Because of what you will learn by briefly slipping into another body's story, style, and pace. By leaving your habits and muscle memory, you will experience how this makes you feel, how this makes you perceive, and how this makes you think. Give it a shot. It's fabulously fun and amazingly insightful to become another body's story. While you're at it, slip into another gender's walk, and other ages as well. You'll be amazed by what you will feel and experience.

By briefly playing with how you walk and move, you will begin to physically and psychically experience slipping into another way of seeing what's around you. Your feelings will shift; you will notice things differently. Don't worry about being perfect in your imitation. Striving for perfection will take you away from the experience and put your focus on the wrong thing. It is the spirit of the movement, the gesture, and the signature of another person's walk that will allow you to get a different perspective on how you yourself move, experience, and think. It's fun! Allow yourself to have fun and see what happens. Keep it up for several minutes. Relax into it, play with it, and see where the imitation leads you.

I suggested this exercise to a client who would fly in from Europe to New York to work with me. "But what if someone I know sees me?" he protested. I reminded him that (a) it was dark outside, (b) he was far from home, and (c) the likelihood of anyone noticing was remote. He resisted nonetheless. I felt that for him in particular this exercise would be very helpful in loosening up his style (he tended to be stiff and somewhat judgmental). About three weeks later, I received this text: "I am now following young Japanese girls, old African men, Italian teenage boys. . . . I cannot stop and am having the time of my life. Thank you."

Many clients have reported back that they do this very frequently, as it is not only really fun but an amazing insight into others that they've never been able to experience any other way.

TRY THIS: MINISTRY OF SILLY WALKS (Part Two)

If you're a Monty Python fan, then you know the above reference to John Cleese's sketch and his hysterically funny Silly Walks Department. If not, check it out. If you allowed yourself to do the "Walk Copy" above, you can go even farther with it. Once you've walked another's walk, speed it up, slow it down, really exaggerate it. Take big, absurdly long strides. Follow those with tiny rapid ones. Move the hips and arms in grand motions. These variations and exaggerations will only deepen your awareness of the impact and power of the bottom half of the body upon the upper half. And since this exercise is all about exaggeration, it's another opportunity to see if your judge permits you to play or not. Both of these exercises can increase your ability to feel your signature walk. Playing with habitual movements can reveal if they need to be adjusted, updated, or improved.

HUMOR

Humor is another aspect of the climate of a workplace, and while tricky to navigate, it is another aspect of fun, warmth, and charm. Can one include humor in a presentation? If so, what kind of humor? Off-color jokes, sarcasm, "funny" put-downs—there is a very fine line between funny and mean, and all of the above should be avoided. But humor, the ability to laugh at oneself or a given situation, provides balance and perspective and enables us to detach a bit from the all-important seriousness with which we take ourselves and our work. Laughter is the best de-stressor there is and is good for the body and the soul. It gives a fresh perspective and creates bonds. "Oh, but I'm not funny," people say. "I can't make jokes." I caution all those who lack a good sense of humor not to attempt being a stand-up comic. It will not work. But humor is not about the ability to come up with one-liners. The root of funny is "fun." Humor is a perspective and point of view; it's all about the spirit of how one looks at things.

Life force, gender, humor, point of view, perspective—these are the soft skills of success that cannot be ignored. These are the human traits that build trust, kinship, rapport, and collaboration.

When preparing a presentation, depending on the goals and your audience, it's good practice to think about places where humor can be embedded in your content. How might irony, contrast, surprise, and reversals be inserted as a way to keep things interesting and lively? Keep in mind that warmth and humor manifest style and radiate presence, and these will only increase your ability to connect.

Chapter 4: Standing Tall

Review Exercises

Legs

- **Beach Walk**—experience how environment affects movement
- **Office Walk**—experience how your style of movement adjusts to the environment

Hips

- **Seated Pelvic Tilt**—properly align hips
- **Belly Dance**—hip rotation
- **Open Hips**—increase range of motion, mobility
- **Take a Thought for a Dance**—movement impacts feeling

Feet

- **Feeling Feet**—experience how feet express
- **Centering**—ground oneself
- **Launch**—feel how centering impacts movement
- **Long Step/Short Step**—play with your walk
- **Sitting Tall**—having presence when seated
- **Walk Copy**—embody another's walking style
- **Ministry of Silly Walks**— play, discover how extreme movement changes your state of mind

Exercise Name	Frequency Goal / Actual	Observations	Next Steps
Walk Copy	2x per day	Doing someone else's walk made me feel how little I move my arms	Increase frequency to 4x per day, teach this to my team during next off site team building
	/		
	/		
	/		
	/		
	/		

Center of
Unconscious Gravity

*"Challenges are gifts that force us to search
for a new center of gravity. Don't fight them.
Just find a different way to stand."*

—Oprah Winfrey

BODY CENTERS

Now that you have a richer understanding of the body's influence and signals on multiple levels of feeling, thinking, communicating, and connecting, and before we move on to the nonphysical aspects of presence, I want to explore two more ways of experiencing how your body impacts interactions and connecting. Recall for a moment the centers explored thus far: head, chest, arms/hands, belly, hips, legs/feet. In a perfect world, the energy and expression within us would move through us in a continuous flow from head to feet, with no dominant center. But a perfect world is elusive, and most of us tend to habitually block or express from one center of our body. I call this our *unconscious* center of gravity.

One of my clients is the CEO of a corporation with 40,000 employees. He's brilliant, and all head. When we met, my first impression was of a giant head placed on a tiny torso. It was as though his entire body existed merely to transport his head around. His gestures were very contained, almost nonexistent, as though not to divert any energy from his brain. Having him do the shake-out "Get the Peanut Butter Off" exercise (Chapter 2) was a major ordeal (and a revelation for him!). My client belonged to the category I call *head* people, those for whom all energy, focus, and life seem to emanate from their heads. Their heads may be lifted high, thrust far forward, or move rapidly to scan their surroundings. Or they may hide their heads, with chins tucked downward and voices swallowed. Either way, their heads are their operational center. Do you know any head-centered people? How does manifesting from that center impact how they are perceived? Or how about those for whom the chest is the center? Whether puffed up or sunken, all energy is either trapped or propelled from the chest and shoulder region. Do you know people who operate from the chest region? Do they seem to manifest worry and fear, or expansive warmth and courage, or perhaps grandiosity? How one's energy and movement are restrained or expressed by a given center can have interesting ramifications. Know any belly or hip people—people who, whether tight or expansive, lead from that part of the body? Imagine your boss and ask yourself: from which body center does he or she lead—or conversely, defend or block? Now for the hard part. Which are you?

TRY THIS: CENTER CONTROL TOWERS

By consciously focusing your energy on different centers, you can experience how your mood, point of view, and way of taking in information are affected.

Begin with your head. Come to a standing position and put all your focus on your head. Imagine it is the source of all your energy and power. Imagine it is twice as large as it is in reality. Now take that "huge head" on a walk and observe how being head-centered makes you feel. Confident? Arrogant? Powerful? Showy? Proud? Strong? Smart? There is no right or wrong feeling. There is just the experience, and given each individual's habitual center, shifting to the head will have widely different results. If you are a belly person, shifting to your head may feel absolutely bizarre.

Now shake out all over and release any tension from the above exercise. Let's do the same with the shoulders. Remain standing and imagine all energy, power, even light emanate from your shoulder region. Imagine entering a room and the first thing anyone will notice about you are your amazing, glowing shoulders. They are the most expressive part of your body. Play with them and see how they would express emotions. Walk around as a shoulder-centered person and again ask yourself how that makes you feel. Excited? Proud? Courageous? Strong? Boastful?

This exercise can also be done as though the shoulders are the heaviest, darkest, most burdened part of the body. The head or shoulders can be hidden as shameful and something you want no one to notice. As they collapse and curve inward, this creates an entirely different series of emotions. Try both approaches and observe the impact.

Now shake out and focus on the belly as the most powerful center from which your energy, light, intelligence, and power come. Give yourself a huge, expansive belly that leads and is open. Make it the center of feeling, decision making, love. Take that on a walk. See what it feels like to let the belly lead and what emotions bubble up as a result. And then try the opposite. Make the belly center cut off, tight, hidden, protected. Take that on a walk and explore.

Finally, do the same with the hips and legs. Exaggerate how you swing your hips from side to side. Or play with making your hips completely stiff and immobile. Now the legs. Are they loose and floppy or hard, stiff, and stomping?

Why explore body centers as described above? By exaggerating each center, you may discover the impact that your habitual body center has on how you communicate, interact, present, and connect. Are you a head-centered or belly-centered person? Do you even know? Ask someone close to you what he or she thinks you are. How does your center affect how you're perceived and how you perceive others in any given situation? Most likely, you are a combination; most of us are. Or perhaps you shift centers according to different circumstances. This is a fascinating line of inquiry and exploration. Go beyond yourself and observe others more closely. Where are your reports' centers? Does your manager's center change in different situations? What center does your friendliest colleague have, or from where does your most challenging coworker lead? How do their centers impact their communication? When one center or area of the body dominates, there is information to be gleaned. Is there resonance or friction between others' centers and yours? Might that explain either rapport or conflict?

My CEO client, who was so head-centric, found that when he explored shifting to his belly, he felt as though he could listen more patiently to his senior leadership team. "I don't know how to explain it," he said to me one day. "But shifting from my head to my belly relaxes me. It lets me allow others to come to their own conclusions without me driving things all the time." That was a big shift in his leadership style, and it rippled throughout his entire team.

TRY THIS: HAPPY SHOULDERS/SAD HIPS

This exercise, like all the others suggested in Part I, is designed to create a *conversation between you and your body*. It offers ways to more deeply experience the complex and amazing interplay between your self and the body that houses that self. By experiencing your body in unusual ways (shifting centers, copying walks, softening the belly), you can more consciously appreciate the powerful instrument in which you live. You can also explore how by making these subtle shifts they impact your communication, and how you experience the world. There are no correct or incorrect ways to play; there is merely the willingness to do so. Are you willing to play? This exercise is meant to explore and feel contradictory emotions in different parts of the body simultaneously. For example, begin by moving your shoulders and feet as if they are both happy and see what that feels like. Rest. Now move the feet as if they are happy and combine that with sad shoulders. Below is a list of a few combinations. Feel free to make up your own and experiment.

Sad feet with happy shoulders
Happy belly with worried head
Happy head with worried belly
Angry feet with happy head
Angry head with angry feet
Happy belly, happy feet

There is no correct or incorrect way to play this exercise. Akin to the "Ministry of Silly Walks," whether or not you give yourself permission to do this exercise, you'll learn something new about yourself and how movement, energy, centers impact your experience of others and yourself.

TRY THIS: HAPPY SHOULDERS/SAD FEET WHILE PRESENTING

To more consciously experience how these centers impact communication, pick one from the above list, stand, and deliver a presentation you have given in the past. What happens? Is the information itself transformed by the movement? Do some aspects of the content seem more or less relevant when delivered by, for example, an angry head? Experiment with a couple of the pairings above using content with which you are very familiar. That way, you can experience how a modification of the instrument radically shifts the impact of the content. You can do this in a very exaggerated way at the start and then allow the movements to become increasingly subtle. Explore what that does to the importance, urgency, and subtext of the content.

WHAT ANIMALS ARE AROUND?

In literature and fairy tales, characters are often given characteristics reminiscent of animals—the wise old owl, the timid sheep, the scaredy-cat. By consciously playing with the idea, "What animal is this person?," different strategies for communicating, managing, and negotiating can be employed. If you engage with a snake in the grass the same way you would a puppy, you are only putting yourself at risk. There is the lone wolf, who works best on his or her own, or the dolphin, definitely a pod person who prefers and is stimulated by collaboration. And of course we may be mixtures of different animals, a wolf on some projects or times of day and a dolphin at others.

Which are you? If you are a puppy and need lots of chew toys and playtime, it's best not to seek an environment filled with old lumbering bears. Why think of yourself or others in this way? Because even though we are all individuals, we are also, as much as we may not like to admit it, types. Anyone who has ever taken a personality test knows how shocking it is to see how seemingly unique individuals fit into just a few personality types. We are all mixtures of various traits. By understanding your overall character (animal) type, it becomes a bit easier to anticipate how you typically respond to challenges. Thinking of other types in this way can provide insight into how to communicate with those who are indeed a different species.

TRY THIS: LIONS, TIGERS, BEARS, . . . AND PUPPIES (Part One)

Look at either an upcoming business challenge, negotiation, or team project and think about what strategies you might employ as you identify which animals your counterparts are. How might you strategize and plan for the turtle in the group? (Lots of quiet and adequate time to get things done.) The shark? (Enough food to keep it sated?) Or the peacock? (Exposure that flatters and shows off his or her beauty!) Seals, vultures, pussycats, elephants, spiders! This is purely imaginary, but it has great application for finding the right approach and tactics for particular people and assignments.

TRY THIS: YOUR INNER ANIMAL (Part Two)

And yourself? Are you a bear or a hummingbird? Each has such wildly different needs, and it might be good to imagine yourself as the animal that reigns deep within to make sure it's getting all it needs and wants. Make a list of those needs. Ask yourself how many are being actualized at work. What might you do to get projects or make changes that are more suited to your animal?

CALM IS CATCHING

Whether copying a walk, exaggerating a center, smiling, or frowning, by simply allowing yourself to experience the extraordinary plasticity, flexibility, and receptivity of the body in which you live, you can experience the profound and constant interplay between the physical and the emotional, perceptual, and ideational. More critical, your body does not operate in isolation. It's not merely for yourself that stress, physical tension, or habitual patterns should be managed. These physical manifestations impede connection and potentially destabilize communication randomly with others *all around you.* Your awareness that there is a mutually regulating system of bodies affecting other bodies makes it all the more crucial to master your own.

There is nothing quite akin to the opening night of a play. Stress couldn't be higher; but actors love and crave the adrenalin that floods their bodies. They've spent years learning how to use and focus that heightened energy. Competitive athletes and others who work under extreme stress understand the power of focus. That's why pilots do endless hours of flight simulator practice, so that if and when a genuine emergency does happen, they'll know how to conquer the stress response and communicate calmly and effectively. But guess what? Presenting, even internally to senior management, can feel as high stakes as opening night.

Recently, I ran backstage to congratulate a TED speaker I'd coached, who in a former life had been a professional sprinter. He'd done a remarkable job. His talk was smooth, effortless, in the moment, and connected. In our rehearsals, he was very open to any suggestions I made. When I pointed out to him that he constantly shifted his weight, swaying from left to right, he had no idea he was doing it. Once I got him to center, grip his toes, and engage his quads, he could feel the impulse to sway and he stopped it before it took over. (Similar to those who have an unconscious repetitive habit, I had him begin to speak, and as he began to sway I put my hands on his hips to stop him. Only by experiencing the cessation was he able for the first time to feel the habit.) After his talk, I asked him how he felt. Even though he'd just walked off stage seconds before, he confessed that he couldn't remember one single moment of what he'd just done. (He did, however, recall that he'd been able to not sway despite his body *really* wanting to.) I was a bit surprised that he couldn't recall what he'd just accomplished. But as a highly trained athlete, he'd spent years learning how to master his adrenaline rush so that he could race like a thoroughbred, tune out everything except the finish line and the clock, and stay calm. At TED his previous athletic training came back, and his focused, calm body took him elegantly through and beyond the finish line of his talk. All this happened despite his mind not recalling a single second of it. Why? He "focused out."

FOCUSING OUT

Shifting your focus and attention away from yourself onto anything outside the self is a terrific stress reducer. Focusing on other people has the added benefit, beyond stress reduction, of increased awareness of the signals being sent. Since most communication is nonverbal, being highly attuned to nonverbal signals only increases one's ability to navigate the unspoken. By focusing outward, those around you will feel and be seen, which is critical for connecting. Another reason to focus outward? Excessive self-focus tends to inhibit spontaneity, ease, and comfort.

TRY THIS: TAKE IT ALL IN

At a meeting, take time to observe what everyone is wearing: shoes, ties, jewelry, accessories of all sorts. Next observe how everyone is sitting. Focus on such things as who is right- or left-handed, who writes with a fountain pen or ballpoint. Just take in all possible data on the visual plane. Look for anything red or green in the room. The fabric of the chairs. If you tend to get nervous, observe if, by focusing your attention on details, you begin to calm down and relax. While this practice is excellent for dealing with nerves, it has the far deeper application that the better one gets at reading a room, the more skillful one becomes at managing it. Surface observations become second nature, and more subtle cues become more easily observed.

TRY THIS: FOCUS ON

This exercise is designed to make you aware of what happens in the body when you are deeply concentrating on something. There are any number of activities you can do to experience focus, so I'll suggest a few simple ones to start, but feel free to make up your own. Grab a pen or pencil and a blank sheet of paper and scribble a random doodle or design on the paper. Now get a pair of scissors and cut as perfectly as possible along the outermost edges of the design. When you are about halfway through, check in and notice what your body feels like when you are completely absorbed in that action. Here's another one: Get a needle and thread, and thread the needle. Then begin to sew along the remainder of the design you drew. Again notice what you feel, how you are breathing, if you are tense, where are you tense? Experience what non–self-centered focus feels like.

TRY THIS: FOCUS ON WHILE PRESENTING

If you have an upcoming presentation about which you're nervous, while rehearsing do one or both of the above activities while speaking the content aloud. Notice what happens when you focus on something outside yourself. Do you stop speaking? Do you lose your train of thought? Can you focus deeply on a physical action while simultaneously delivering your content? Developing the mental skill to focus out while simultaneously communicating without losing your place is a goal to work toward.

TRY THIS: SAFE-PLACE SENSE MEMORY

This exercise is more of an ongoing practice than a one-time tip. If you incorporate it into your life and return to it frequently, it will engender a state of centered calm that you can access in an instant. For the initial practice of this exercise, allow at least 10 to 15 minutes. Anyone whose professional role is highly stressful, but cannot appear as such, may find great benefit from "Safe-Place Sense Memory."

Find a comfortable place to sit. Relax the body, close your eyes, and picture a place that you genuinely love and in which you feel *completely safe*. It can be a favorite room or someplace outside. It can be from your youth or a place you go on vacation. No matter where, just imagining it quickly sheds layers of tension. While you sit there, imagine or recall as best you can what is to your left, what is to your right, what's in front of and behind you, and what is above and below you. Fill in as many details as possible, every aspect of the place in every direction. Don't rush through this, as you'll keep remembering more details the longer you focus on each area. Beyond what you can see, how does the air feel? Is it dry or humid? Still or breezy? What is the temperature? Is it cool, warm, hot, cold? What is the time of day? What is the quality of light? What sounds are there? What does it smell like? Use *each sense* to complete your mental immersion in the place. Again, initially give yourself a good 10 to 15 minutes to accomplish just this part of the exercise. When practiced routinely, the calm, focused centeredness this exercise engenders can be found in just moments. But you have to practice it and perfect it. Check in with the body now and feel the centered calm it possesses. Open your eyes, stand, and walk around. Observe how that feeling impacts your movements. Calm authority resonates outward like ripples in a pond. It is yours to access, connect with, and spread.

Some clients have found benefit by adding one final step to this exercise. Once they are mentally inside the place of calm, they pick an object—it can be a small stone or piece of jewelry—and they imbue that object with the spirit of the place of calm. They then carry that object in a pocket, and when nervous or worried, they touch the stone as a way to reconnect with that centered calmness. The traditions of sacred talismans, worry beads, and rosaries are examples of how just being in contact with an object imbued with meaning can calm a racing heart.

The above exercises, in combination with the breathing and centering exercises, can and should be used before any high-stakes communication. Calm is catching, focus is riveting, and mastery of one's adrenaline response is essential for the content inside your head to be embedded in your audiences' heads. I'll repeat my favorite new saying: practice doesn't make perfect; it makes imperfection livable. Great communicators practice. A lot.

As we all know, the body is a deeply interconnected system. No system is separate, and each impacts the others. Nonetheless, it is my hope that by having explored some of the suggested exercises, you've gotten to experience how even the slightest adjustment in one part of the body can have a profound impact on how you connect, what you communicate, and what others experience of you. We are, at all times, both senders and receivers of complex signals in the present. The next chapter will focus on presence, how it influences who we are, how we are perceived, and how we can be flexible in an ever-shifting now.

Chapter 5: Center of Unconscious Gravity

Review Exercises

- **Center Control Towers**—experience shifting centers
- **Happy Shoulders/Sad Hips**—movement and emotion
- **Happy Shoulders/Sad Feet While Presenting**—how movement changes meaning
- **Lions, Tigers, Bears, . . . and Puppies**—managing different personalities
- **Your Inner Animal**—knowing your style needs
- **Take It All In**—focus, calm nervous energy
- **Focus On**—deeper concentration
- **Focus On While Presenting**—dual focus for concentration
- **Safe-Place Sense Memory**—accessing inner calm

Exercise Name	Frequency Goal / Actual	Observations	Next Steps
Take It All In	2x per day; 5 minutes at a time	Realize how much I miss	Take in "people" not just objects, increase amount I do this
	/		
	/		
	/		
	/		
	/		

PART II

PRESENCE IS A SKILL NOT A GIFT

Presence

"Presence. That will definitely cost you more."

—Anonymous headhunter

At an executive leadership workshop I was offering at a large corporation, the company's chief legal counsel stood up to make a few introductory remarks. She reported that while talking to a recruiter, she listed all the skills and areas of expertise she wanted in her next hire. At the end she listed presence as a vital quality she was expecting. "Well," said the recruiter. "Presence. That will *definitely* cost you more." Presence, that ineffable thing, is itself a commodity. But what exactly is it?

My client, Theo, had been with his company for decades. His company had grown from a few hundred employees when he started to over 40,000 worldwide. He came to see me because he was transitioning from a role where he had literally hundreds of dotted line reports and over 20 direct to a position where he had zero. For his new role, he had to travel the world and meet with CEOs and high government officials as an emissary and champion of his organization. The role was both an honor and an imposition; he wasn't looking forward to it. "In the past, at least I had the carrot and the stick as a way to influence and engage the troops. Now what have I got?"

The first thing I noticed about Theo was how exhausted he looked. His voice was thin and scratchy, his face aloof, his posture weak. As he sat in my office, his right arm rested on his right leg, and his left arm was crossed over his whole body to rest on the *right* arm of his chair. He was curled up like a pretzel and stayed like that, crossed and covering the center of his body, for a full 45 minutes. There he sat, twisted up, his energy dull and tired, his voice a droning monotone. "I'm not ready to retire, but I know this position has characteristically meant the end of the game."

I listened to his words, the doubt, and the worry, but mostly I observed his body. Near the end of our first meeting, I asked if he might consider moving his left arm so that it rested on the left armrest, rather than on the one all the way across his body.

"What difference would *that* make?" he snapped.

I suggested that by keeping himself all curled up, he looked tired, disengaged, and defensive, and that by opening up his chest region and sitting up, he might appear and actually feel a bit more engaged. He might begin to breathe more deeply as well. He fought me tooth and nail. "All this new age stuff about the body and breathing and empathy. I don't buy a bit of it."

"No need," I countered. "All I'm asking is if you'd move your arm." Reluctantly, he did so. His homework? To be more aware in the moment of his posture, breathing, and movements and to observe if there was any correlation between how he moved and how he felt, how he moved and how others reacted. My last request was for him not to sit all curled up and immobile but to open his chest region and move his arms.

"Well, that's the most patently absurd request I've ever had."

"Ignore it then," I replied. "It's your money!"

"Company's money," he tossed back.

"Fantastic. No worries! It's just merely your time then."

"This way I sit, it is part of my style, almost my brand, I would argue."

"Fine, so be it. But your *brand* is looking quite out-of-date and tired, and for this new role, if you really don't want this to be an exit position, I suggest it's time for a refresh."

Two weeks later Theo returned.

"All right," he began. "I'm going to give you just a tiny amount of credit." He paused. I waited. "As you recommended, I began to move my arms." Another pause. "My wife and daughters made great hash of me, told me I look like a complete phony, waving them about." Pause. "But the funny thing is . . . and what I can't seem to wrap my head around is . . . I'm having new *ideas*."

"It's one system, Theo. We must move beyond the Cartesian model of the mind-body split. Indeed, most contemporary neuroscience put that to rest decades ago."

"But ideas generated from movement?"

"New *patterns* of movement. It's all about breaking old habits and creating new pathways. What are some of those ideas, by the way, if you're willing to share?"

We got into a rather lengthy discussion about time and influence and navigating the present, which led me to tell Theo about the being in the now and my observations of its effects. Again he pushed back with his grave mistrust of anything "new age." "But I like you, Gina, so I'll listen. More than that, I can't promise."

Likability, trust, patience—these are the turnkeys that slowly permit one to push the envelope.

"Well then, let's try an experiment," I countered. "What is the script you use when you go to these meetings with CEOs and government officials around the world?"

"It's a pitch essentially. I've got my 10 minutes of prewritten talking points. I speak it and get the heck out of there as soon as possible."

"Do you feel engaged while doing so?" He laughed at the very idea. "Do you ever let the script go and just go with your gut and let the meeting just happen not according to script?"

"Not if I can help it."

"Why not?"

"That's not the job. The job is to get into the room, do my bit, exchange cards, and call it a day."

"No wonder it's an exit position."

"Well, what are you suggesting I do?"

"I'm not suggesting anything. I'm just asking if what you are doing suits not only the job, but the moment. The unique moment that you have with each encounter. To me, what you're describing sounds as pointless as insisting on driving straight on a road that's full of curves. You have to adjust your style according to what each encounter demands."

There was a long silence. Theo looked quite lost. Finally, he said, "I don't follow. I follow the bit about the road, but that's not really analogous, is it?"

"Isn't it?" I then told Theo about the Rule of the Yes from improvisation.

THE RULE OF THE YES

When actors improvise, they often do so with no props. Everything is conjured in the immediate moment, invisibly. In an improvisation, no one knows what is coming next. When one actor holds out an invisible something to the other, that second actor will probably already have a flicker of something in mind, because it's quite scary to stand onstage before an audience and not have *any* idea of what is going to happen. The mind instinctively conjures up ideas. Suddenly the first actor says, "Here's a lovely birthday cake I made for you." And the second actor, the respondent, who might have been expecting an imaginary set of keys or a cell phone, must instantaneously adjust and let that first imagined thought go. Why? Because the first law of improvisation is to never deny another's established reality. If actor number two were to reply, "There's no cake in your hands," the improvisation, like a popped balloon, would instantly deflate into meaninglessness. What the Rule of the Yes does is immediately create a common ground upon which the actors can walk, moment by unexpected moment, constantly remaking the reality by adding on to and accepting each other's unfolding imaginary world.

Why might any professional benefit from this rule? The simple fact is that every encounter, every sales call, every negotiation is an improvisation. No one knows going in how it will end. Those who are present must constantly reset their expectations, recalibrate to suit the exigencies of the moment. How often after a meeting has gone south did you in hindsight realize, "Damn! That moment when he looked at his watch and put his hands on the conference table as if to say, 'This is over,' and I kept talking and talking. That's when I blew it." (That's providing you do a postmortem. Do you? If not, I highly recommend regularly doing so.)

The biggest difference between actors and nonactors is that the former spend years in training *to unlearn* the blocks that jam up the flow. That's how they develop presence. That commodity. Successful salespeople learn this over time, or somehow instinctively know it, but the conscious development of this skill as a key component of presence itself is rarely taught. (I once worked with someone who'd spent a few years in the CIA. One of the earliest trainings he had to take covered how to become invisible, to not have any presence, to be someone no one would ever remember meeting. Now he was a tall, charming, very handsome young man, and he had to transform himself into someone no one would ever recall. He was proof of point if one can learn how to become invisible, one can certainly learn and master its opposite!)

Back to Theo. He listened and acknowledged that in theory he could understand the value of the Rule of the Yes for theater, but in real life it was not applicable. In the kinds of meetings he had, meetings that sometimes took months to arrange, there were expectations that had to be met. He couldn't simply ignore the objectives and go with the flow; it would be foolish, risky, and unproductive.

Convincing individuals of something about which they have strong objections is not my goal. Rather, I attempt to introduce a different way of looking at a problem. In that spirit, I suggested to Theo that his point of view about the meetings was counterproductive and his behavior during them was creating missed opportunities time and again.

"Missed how?"

"Missed because *you* are not there. You are a mouthpiece, spouting predetermined, prewritten text. They might as well just send a robot! By not allowing yourself to go with whatever the opportunity presents, you are essentially obeying the rule of the no." He looked at me for a long time but said nothing.

Many think presence is a kind of innate charisma, a quickness, a glow, a vitality, and either you've got it or you don't; you're born with it or you're not. When asked to define it, words like *confidence, aura,* and *energy* top the list. Digging deeper to understand how those qualities are made manifest, such things as posture and eye contact are suggested. Indeed, all the physical aspects discussed in Part I are the building blocks of presence. But then there is this question of the present moment itself, the constantly changing, never static *isness* of multilayered reality. I recall reading that according to Buddhist thought, at any given moment, we have 3,000 possible reactions. Second by unfolding second, 3,000 options! I've no idea how that particular number was arrived at, and who knows, maybe it's 300,000 or 3 million options. The point is, moment by moment, we live at the edge of time, and the possibilities for how we choose to react are infinite. That is the most crucial aspect of presence, one's flexibility with and effortless management of an ever-changing now. The ability to navigate the present moment is not an innate secret gift or mystery. As someone who's spent years teaching actors how to attain presence, I know with absolute certainty that it is a teachable skill. Presence is the result of a series of actions. It is the situational alignment of how one moves, speaks, thinks, listens *in* the present moment combined with the *undoing of blocks that keep us removed from our impulses.*

Theo returned a few weeks later from a trip to Singapore where he'd gone to meet a head of state. The flight from New York was almost 24 hours long; the assumption had been that the meeting would last a mere 15 minutes and he'd be back on a plane later that day.

"I have a gift for you," he said. I looked around for a nicely wrapped box but saw none.

"You shouldn't have."

"The man I was supposed to meet kept me waiting for over an hour. When I entered his office, he was in a fit about some deal that had gone bad. He literally was ranting and raving. I sat there, none too pleased myself, let me tell you, what with the long flight, the long wait, and now his outrageous performance. I thought of you and what you said about forgetting the script and going with whatever was happening. Ordinarily I would have just politely waited, done my bit, and left; but since all else was so off kilter I decided to 'go with the moment.'

I was tired of putting up with his behavior, so I just blurted out 'It's a fucking crying shame, isn't it?' He stopped. It was as though he just realized I was in the room. I held my breath because I had no idea if he'd get even more angry, but by then I really didn't give a damn. Instead, he laughed. Somehow, my going with my impulse, as you would call it, made him laugh. It was as though he realized how absurd his behavior had been. We talked for the next hour and a half. It was amazing! We're doing business."

"'Cause you were real. You were present."

"I guess."

"Thanks for the gift. I'll treasure it."

The transformation of Theo was akin to watching a withered plant in desperate need of water slowly coming back into green vibrance. What was most wonderful about our time working together was, despite our almost universal disagreement about most things—political, intellectual, societal—we connected experientially. We were able to completely bypass the usual barriers to trust and engage fully in the moment together. I attribute this in no small part to *my* lifetime practice of doing the "flow."

THE FLOW

"The Flow" is an exercise that asks the practitioner to speak aloud the stream of thoughts, whether flowing or clogged, running through his or her mind as he or she performs any simple but focused task. It's quite unnerving and extremely difficult because that stream, which goes on continually inside each of us, is quieted very early in our development by socialization: parents, school, life. Indeed, those who don't repress the wild ride inside and speak it aloud are considered mad.

For decades I taught the flow to my acting students and patiently observed as they attempted to dip into the rushing river of their thoughts. The flow puts one into that constant stream and asks that he or she say out loud all that pops up in front of an audience. In their first attempts most actors would say one or two very obvious and superficial things, such as "I'm standing here." And then they would become quiet for a very long time. Everyone's quiet place is unique, as it relates to the specific taboos that were imposed from very early on. But eventually, when feeling safer, something true would pop out. Similar to a dam under tremendous pressure breaking open, words would just pour out. Thoughts, images, sensations, feelings, fears, hopes, jokes, whatever was zooming about inside the head would be liberated. The transition from long silences to uncensored thoughts being spoken could be sudden or painstaking. It all depended upon the person. But once liberated, it would become an unstoppable force. Universally, the response from both speaker and observer was the same. Irrespective of culture, politics, gender, race, age, religion, ethnicity, talent, when the speaker finally tapped into his or her uncensored thoughts and let the truth flow, it was a revelation. Every person in the room would be riveted. Spellbound. For decades I got to experience over and over the absolute magic and power of revealed truth. What an honor and gift it was to help each person's truth emerge. I had students from every walk of life, every shade of skin, every social and economic class, every sexual orientation. I had students from the Caribbean; Latin America; Asia; Europe; north, south, urban, and rural United States; and Canada. None of those identifiers mattered a hoot when the actor rode the flow. Every time the audience would be breathless, silent, enraptured. Why? Because truth revealed, no matter how messy and uncomfortable, no matter how distant from the audience's own experience or point of view, is captivating. The muscle and courage it takes to break open that dam of self and reveal it captures the human heart utterly. We cannot look away. Quite the opposite, it compels our attention.

In what way can an exercise like the flow have meaning for people in business who would never be asked to perform such a task? How can those who do not need or want to open up their endless stream of inner chatter to the outside world apply the lessons of the flow? Why would they? In reality, one needs merely to hear it *internally* and acknowledge it, not necessarily speak it out loud. But the process of actually speaking it has tremendous impact. Why? Because what the exercise does is open up what one prefers to hide and expose it to the light. Why would anyone be crazy enough do this? For the simple reason that the pressure to bury one's true self is much more depleting than bringing it out into the open. We all have our personal places of embarrassment or shame that we spend vast amounts of time trying to conceal. But once exposed, they're usually not such a big deal at all! Actors need to do this for the simple reason that it permits them to discover their unique impulses, for it is precisely the specificity of each actor's impulses that differentiates how he or she interprets a role.

Going back to earlier in this book, think of all the examples of ways people attempted to physically hide something about which they were self-conscious or ashamed and how that impacted their communication: mumbled, inaudible speech to hide insecurity about one's knowledge or skill set, hands that hide a weak chin, crunching down to hide one's height. None of these are that far off from other attempts to hide deeper aspects of one's "shameful" self. Trustworthiness, connection, and the success of ensuing business relationships can often be directly linked to how comfortable and accepting of yourself you are.

While presenting, when meeting a new client, when speaking up before senior management, the courage to go off script, to freely associate to a new idea, to speak a thought that suddenly occurs, all depend on your ability to access those unexpected associations and ideas, to have sufficient "presence of mind" to decide whether or not to verbalize the unexpected. When in a meeting, how confidently someone leaps into the fray, offers ideas, counters group-think—all these actions derive from managing the inner flow.

TRY THIS: THE FLOW: A TOE IN THE STREAM

Sit in a comfortable chair and begin by just noticing what your five senses are taking in around you. After a few moments of silent observation, begin to say out loud first what you see around you. Then jump to what you hear. Full sentences are not needed, just words or phrases that capture what's present. Go to smell, and if there is a smell, describe it briefly. Just a few words. Touch with your hand the surface of the seat you're sitting on and describe it, again briefly. Bring your attention to your mouth; do you taste anything? Go sense by sense and then circle back to sight, hearing, smell, touch, taste. After a round or two, allow whatever sense is most attuned in the moment to tell you what to say or briefly focus on. Try this for three minutes or so. Notice when or if you become silent. If that happens, just go back to one of the senses and say out loud what it notices.

TRY THIS: THE FLOW: BODY *NOW*

After noticing and speaking what the five senses are observing, notice how your body feels. It may be something as simple as observing how you're sitting, if your foot fell asleep, or if your arm itches. Just say aloud whatever physical sensations you notice.

TRY THIS: THE FLOW: MIND *NOW*

Carrying forward and building upon the first two steps, now notice if the mind goes elsewhere, a memory, an association, a fear, a wish, a desire—whatever pops up, permit yourself to speak it. Again, full sentences aren't necessary. A name, a word, anything that captures the fleeting thought before it morphs into the next is enough. If you become silent, when you notice it, go back to a sense and just begin to speak out loud what that sense is observing. The goal is to notice and ride the endless stream of thought out loud.

I've spent decades not only teaching the exercise but doing it myself. What I've discovered is that even if just one person in a pair is awake to the inner stream of impressions, associations, memories, and fears, that capacity somehow, mysteriously, almost magically *unlocks it in the other*. The combined practices of "Soft Belly" (Chapter 3), "The Flow" (variations above), and "Elephant Ears" (Chapter 1), which *all of us* can do *any time*, enable connection irrespective of opinion. One's ability and comfort with jumping fully into the moment, not knowing or having an agenda but following the flow of thoughts and impressions, daring to speak the difficult with compassion and humor, evoke similar behavior from those with whom one is relating. I want to emphasize again that these are not special talents. *All of us have the ability to be present, to risk, to intuit, and to be fully awake to what the moment offers.* It is the process of discovering *the filters that prevent such engagement* that requires attention, focus, and practice. Presence is the courage to dive into the moment before you, to live on the razor-edge of time.

Theo dared to speak up to the man in Singapore because he'd experienced several months of being in the now *with* me. He experienced that he'd not only survived but thrived. He was willing to bring that newfound trust in his own ability to be in the present into another circumstance, thereby bringing along a complete stranger into *that* present moment. Whether you are a CEO in Germany, a financial analyst in Australia, or a kindergarten teacher in Savannah, what enables you to get what's in your brain into the brains of your audience, while completely idiosyncratic, is totally universal. Both are rooted in the truth of the present moment, just like the flow. What dams up the flow and keeps us removed from that present is fear of failure or the parts of ourselves we are ashamed of and feel we need to hide.

DARE TO FAIL

At a Broadway show I was attending, the set was a kitchen, with a high shelf that went along the walls and had vases and baskets all along it. Upon an actor's entrance, a vase fell off the shelf and went rolling on the floor. The actor did nothing. He froze. The audience watched the vase rolling . . . and rolling . . . and rolling . . . because, sadly, that became the most truthful moment on stage. Meanwhile the play stopped dead in its tracks. Finally, after several seconds, another actor walked over, picked up the vase, and placed it on a table, just as one would in real life! Like a key turned in an ignition, the play started up again. (Not surprisingly, that's all I recall of the entire production.) One might characterize the vase falling as a failure, as it broke the illusion. But the vase falling was not the problem; these things happen. *It was the actor's inability to deal with it that was the tipping point.*

How to embed presence and moment-to-moment flow when giving a presentation will be covered in greater depth in the following chapter on design, but a key take-away is to never attempt to ignore or hide any slip-up or technical glitch. Audiences are very smart; they will catch these things. Remember, they are on your side. Acknowledge, use, breathe through any mishap, and you will instantly gain an audience's trust as someone who has enough leadership presence to handle the unexpected.

In general, almost all of us will do anything to avoid failure. But it is also our opinion about what constitutes failure that needs constant revision. I've had many experiences in the theater, as both audience member and performer, where a mess-up not only more deeply engaged the audience but opened up new possibilities for how to improve a scene. There's an expression in the theater called "use it," meaning embrace whatever mess-up happens, incorporate it rather than avoid it or pretend it didn't occur. When you try to avoid or hide mistakes, all truth goes out the window, and the bond between audience and actor is broken. This echoes my previous statement regarding practice making imperfection livable. In the workplace, one's credibility and trustworthiness become suspect by any attempt to cover up one's mistakes.

When I was teaching acting, I had my students write on the covers of their notebooks, "Dare to fail." That was the mantra. Dare to fail: big, publicly, and to do it again and again. The expression "You don't need courage in a field of daisies" acknowledges the truth that it is through hardship and failure that we grow skills, muscle, and resolve. But to actively embrace failure as a mode of learning is in direct opposition to almost all education, especially in our early and very character-forming years. Younger students are not encouraged to fail; rather, in test after test after test, they are taught to avoid failure at all costs. Mistakes become anathema, humiliating, things to hide or cover up. And yet every scientist knows that failure is the key to discovery. Every athlete knows that a lost game or race is an opportunity to further refine technique. Every actor knows that failure is almost always the result of playing "at" the role, rather than "living" inside it, being stuck in one's head rather than jumping with both feet into an impulse. Even if that impulse turns out not to be the proper choice, for any number of reasons, more is discovered by failing than by playing it safe. What can business learn from this, and how can other professionals change their points of view and even definitions of failure?

After years of acting and teaching, I felt the need to stretch my skills, so I took a clown workshop. I had no desire to become a clown, but I wanted to understand and experience something out of my comfort zone. The workshop was taught by a gifted actress and director who had studied in France at the famous Jacques Lecoq school. The students were professional actors who, like me, wished to explore another approach to performance and gain new techniques. The workshop was not about juggling or making silly pratfalls on banana peels; it was about creating what's called a personal clown, a character-driven entity more like a Charlie Chaplin than a red-nosed circus clown (although we did wear red noses for a while, which was a wonderful surprise, an automatic entry into another reality!).

For the first exercise, each of us was told to get onstage one by one and make the class of 25 strangers laugh. While sitting in the audience, we'd watch as our classmates would do practically anything to evoke laughter; we'd imagine our own schemes, certain that we would be the one to draw howls of laughter. Not a single one of us was able to make the audience even snicker. Dead silence greeted every effort. We all failed *miserably*, and we all got to watch each other fail miserably. If the teacher had told us ahead of time that that was the point of the exercise, most might have quit the class on the spot. She saved that insight until all 25 of us had had the experience—and survived it.

What was the point of that exercise? The essence of character clown, as she then explained, is that you will do positively *anything* for love and acceptance. Anything. That the feelings of terror, failure, loneliness, vulnerability that each of us so acutely experienced were the seeds from which our personal "character" clown would germinate. Once she explained the soul around which we would build our characters, failure was embraced. Over and over, in task after task, failure actually became the goal. Instead of something utterly humiliating and to be avoided at all costs, we all strove to completely mess up. What a revelation! What freedom emerged. Add a red nose and a costume to that state of pure need, and every clown became irresistible and unimaginably funny.

What relevance has this to professionals where failure is neither an option nor something to pursue? A lot.

TRY THIS: THE SEED OF FAILURE (Part One)

Think back to something you did long ago that you consider to have been a professional failure. Write down precisely what made it a failure. Was it your skill level at the time, your emotional immaturity, circumstances beyond your control?

TRY THIS: WHAT DID FAILURE GROW? (Part Two)

What were the personal, financial, professional outcomes of that failure? Write them down. Now leap ahead in time mentally and ask yourself what were the long-term effects and learnings that were *engendered* by that failure? In general, not always but usually upon review, people realize that the failure, so painful or humiliating at the time it happened, resulted in positive outcomes over time. Something completely unexpected was learned. Or due to a prior failure, a similar mistake was avoided. We grow from failure. Plain and simple. Over and over, our lives are the accumulation of random inexplicable events for which we have little or no experience except our previous failures!

TRY THIS: FAILURE'S OFFSPRING (Part Three)

Now take a more recent event that you feel was far from successful and ask yourself what might be the outcome a month, six months, or a year from now. Imagine failure not as something to avoid or feel ashamed about but as an opening to possibility.

OWN IT

In any profession, ownership of one's mistakes is vital. Increasingly, people pass the blame rather than own up to their faulty judgments. Those who say, "I did it, I messed up, I'm sorry, and I'll do whatever possible to fix it," seem to be the exception. (Or conversely, apologizing comes too easily. "I'm sorry" is said, but that's the end of it. No solution is offered regarding how to clean up the mess.) These days, whether in politics or boardrooms, the virus of passing the buck and actively refusing to take responsibility for one's mistakes is emblematic of infantilism run rampant. That's what three-year-olds do! "He *made* me do it" is a cry every parent or preschool teacher has heard innumerable times. How different is that from "My admin messed up," "My colleague didn't get me the files on time," or "My computer crashed"? Own your mistakes, admit to them, and communicate possible solutions! If you do so, you will only increase your leadership presence and gain more respect from your colleagues. These are such basic rules of the social contract, it is stunning that they even need to be stated. But I am continually amazed by how quickly people are willing to pass the blame rather than own up to their own mistakes.

Failure is obviously something most wish to avoid. But for many, success is even scarier. Many people are more comfortable with the self-limiting results of old habits. For them, the risks that full engagement with the present can unleash are just too much. Why might that be? With success comes increased responsibility and visibility, as well as greater exposure to risk and unpredictable unknowns. There's a Dutch saying, "The tall trees get the wind." In essence it means, with increased responsibility comes greater vulnerability to the unexpected. Navigating the unexpected requires flexibility and courage. For some, it is easier to stay within a narrower range of risk, visibility, and responsibility. What's most critical is to know your own tolerance for stress and exposure. Not everyone has to be a tall tree! But it is vital to determine if it is fear of failure or fear of success that hobbles risk taking. Whether of failure or success, you can be certain fear will impact how you communicate in high-stakes and day-to-day exchanges.

TRY THIS: WHAT IF . . . ?

Write down an aspiration that you hold dear: getting that promotion you desire or that project you want to work on. Now list all the possible pitfalls that might occur as a result of achieving that aspiration. Next write down all the advantages or opportunities that may come of it. Read both lists and ask yourself (and notice what your belly feels) if you are more unnerved by the list of risks or opportunities.

All of us have people from our personal and professional lives whom we look up to and admire. They may not even be people we know. They can be a great person from history, politics, sports, the arts, or just a close relative. Often someone is admired because he or she manifests one's own aspirations and values. From one's perspective, those heroes lived their values fully and boldly. For those who worry about failing, presenting, or even communicating in general, it can be a great exercise to imagine their hero and communicate to him or her in a safe, imaginary context.

TRY THIS: WRITE YOUR HERO A LETTER

When there is a difficult decision to be made, write your hero a letter asking for his or her thoughts and opinions. Let the letter fully express your ideas and concerns. Following that exercise—and here's the fun part—have your hero write you back with his or her ideas. This exercise is a wonderful way to access a part of the self that is nascent and wants to emerge. Also, I recommend doing this exercise with a pen and paper and not on a computer. There is something inexplicably personal about using the hand in that way that feels wonderful, slow, and true.

TRY THIS: BE YOUR HERO

If you are wrestling with a challenge or are very nervous about an upcoming business deal, or risk, or presentation, close your eyes and imagine your hero. Hear his or her voice; imagine how he or she walks, gestures, and moves. After a few moments, still with your eyes closed, come to a standing position and imagine you *are* your hero. Open your eyes and slowly move about the room; look around; embody the hero's pace, style, posture, gestures, and presence. Begin to speak the presentation, business idea, or risk aloud, as though you are your hero. Explore how the imaginary embodiment makes you feel. When attempting to garner new ideas or support for an upcoming challenge, observe if by moving like your hero, different thoughts and solutions bubble up from this imaginary embodiment. If nothing pops up, that's fine. If nothing else, it's just fun to pretend!

The mind is a rich tapestry of impulses, sensations, thoughts, reactions, memories, associations, perceptions, all in constant flux and flow. For many, stream of consciousness feels less like a stream and more like a congested road full of random vehicles going in opposite directions. Intrusive, disruptive, negative thoughts can seemingly pop up out of nowhere. Habitual, negative self-dialogue can overwhelm purposeful concentration. Worry, rumination, obsessive thoughts, random associations, the list goes on and on. Psychologists, philosophers, neuroscientists, and the clergy all attempt to unravel these mysteries from their own perspectives. Regarding communication, it is amazing how those types of thoughts can creep into physical gestures and verbal exchanges. Understanding how thoughts might be focused to impact one's ability to navigate the present moment is still in its infancy. I have no concrete answers, only experiences that have helped me to explore how the mind and imagination, in concert with the body, can be used to break through the blocks that keep us stuck and hinder impactful connection and communication. Do you make a self-sabotaging facial expression or gesture after expressing an idea? Do you sigh loudly to express displeasure? Do you laugh or giggle after expressing an opinion? Do you not communicate an idea because you second-guess yourself? (Some of my clients often report that they are so busy judging what they want to contribute in meetings that by the time they're ready to speak, the subject has changed and conversation has moved on.) Keep in mind that just as you are constantly adding new data points about those with whom you work, they are doing so about you. Presence is an evolving conception in others' experiences of you, as well as your own self-conception. Presence is not fixed. We are all works in progress. Communication is constant, and being completely present in the moment is available to all of us. But like everything else, mastery requires practice.

Chapter 6: Presence

Review Exercises

- **The Flow: A Toe in the Stream**—hearing oneself
- **The Flow: Body _Now_**—physical presence
- **The Flow: Mind _Now_**—thought presence
- **The Seed of Failure**—self review
- **What Did Failure Grow?**—outcomes of past actions
- **Failure's Offspring**—awareness of unexpected outcomes
- **What If . . . ?**—imagination
- **Write Your Hero a Letter**—access your inner smarts, courage
- **Be Your Hero**—exactly!

Exercise Name	Frequency Goal / Actual	Observations	Next Steps
Write Your Hero a Letter	When stuck on a problem	I had the answers but didn't realize it	Do this even when I think I have a solution to see what I discover
	/		
	/		
	/		
	/		

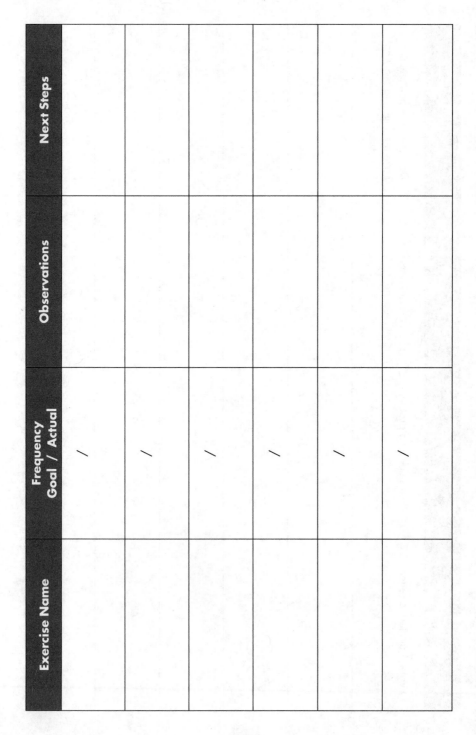

Exercise Name	Frequency Goal / Actual	Observations	Next Steps
	/		
	/		
	/		
	/		
	/		
	/		

Designing Messages to Increase Presence

"Brevity is the soul of wit."

—WILLIAM SHAKESPEARE

One's presence is further established by how communications are structured, designed, and delivered. Content, whether written or spoken, needs to be consistent, concise, and clear. It can be hard to be clear, especially when deeply knowledgeable about the details of a subject. There are a multitude of questions to be answered before delivering information: Who will the audience be? How much complex information should be offered? Will it be a decision-making audience perhaps not well versed in the subject? Essentially, what is the goal of the communication?

To design for enhanced presence and clarity of communication, I recommend key messaging. Key messaging is an excellent brainstorming, problem-solving, presentation tool. It's basically an extension of outlining, which is traditionally taught in middle school, and it's a core concept of media training. It organizes ideas, actions, and results in a way that can be either very lean and high level or quite detailed. It is *very* simple, but it is *not* easy. It takes practice. It's well worth the effort, as its results are extremely effective. It is rooted in the structure of storytelling, and it is through story, not merely data, that we explain the complexities of our world.

I was recently asked by a leader of a large global team of medical statisticians to teach key messaging to his reports. His people not only have to design highly complex clinical trials for new oncology therapies; they need to keep detailed records of the incredibly varied results of those trials. Day in and day out, they swim in an ever rising sea of data, shifting from the granular details of molecular science to meta-analyses of lab results. "Storytelling has nothing to do with us," one man said. "The only thing we care about is statistics."

"I understand," I replied. "But have you ever considered that behind every single number in each statistic there is a story?"

He was unconvinced: "Our results are all that the regulators care about."

"Of course. But the biochemistry of a side effect or the absorption rate of a molecule by the kidney can be communicated in story form as well as statistical, can it not? Tell me how a molecule is targeted to arrive at the specific destination cell of the tumor."

He reluctantly agreed and then went on to briefly and quite eloquently describe the journey of a specific molecular agent as it makes its way from IV drip to cell tumor. The room was enraptured. Even cells make a hero's journey! Numbers can support and provide backup, but numbers and data don't engage. Journeys do.

The biggest challenge to implementing key messaging is sufficient time for proper focus. In our increasingly distracted, multitasking, goal-driven world, it's difficult to carve out the time to sit and think, to get a bird's-eye view of the specific situation that needs to be addressed. Almost all professionals know how to *do* what they do; days are composed of taking action. But I've found over many years of teaching key messaging, it's very difficult for most to define the underlying conditions and influences of those actions, what I call the situational demands—or the *what*. This is easy to understand, as situations are often complex and multilayered. For example, let's use a backache as a "situation." Some obvious causes of a backache may be (1) a pulled muscle, (2) a budging disk, or (3) kidney disease. The job of a good physician is to drill down past the "presenting" symptoms and find the underlying cause of the backache so that appropriate medical action can be taken. The diagnostic tools that doctors employ exist to identify the *what* behind the symptoms. It would be great if all professionals were trained to dig as deeply as physicians into the core of each situation.

In business, for example, a *what* may be a colleague with whom there is friction. From one person's perspective, that would be the presenting symptom. But how is that friction experienced? Is the colleague rude (or too stressed and busy to engage)? Is the colleague competitive (or threatened)? Is the colleague cold (or merely preoccupied)? The first step before taking action is to define the *specificity of the cause behind the manifest behavior*. As should be obvious from this brief example, there may be many complex reasons behind why a colleague acts in certain ways, reasons that may be very personal, or not personal at all. How to diagnose? Accurately attempting to define behavior can prove challenging, but it is well worth the effort. Not doing so would be akin to a doctor prescribing ibuprofen for what might be kidney disease!

The above example focused on symptoms or behaviors, but the *what*, or the situation to be communicated or formally presented, can be any number of things. The *what* can be an innovation, a problem, a challenge, a new client, a business plan, a new product. The *what* is anything that needs to be explored, addressed, communicated, or managed. For example, if the *what* is a burning building, the next step, or the *how*, would be to call the fire department to put out the fire. Finally comes the *why*, which defines the hoped-for results or goals of the actions taken. In the case of a burning building, the *why* is to put out the fire, prevent spread, and save lives and property. Simple, as indicated, but not easy. Here's why.

Regarding the above example, no substantial information about the building itself was given. A fully occupied elementary school in a city versus an old, abandoned barn in the middle of nowhere might require very different actions, or *hows*. For the former, calling the fire department to extinguish the fire is a no-brainer; for the latter, it might make more sense to conduct a controlled burn and demolish an unsafe structure. The actions taken must always be contingent on the situation at hand. In business, most situations are not as obvious as a fire and require nuanced definition and responses. That takes us back to carving out the needed time to fully think through, define, and understand the presenting situation.

Why might such a model as key messaging be so vital for moment-by-moment presence? If you drive, take a minute to recall learning how you did so. It was hard to learn all the aspects of managing your own car, not to mention navigating all possible contingencies of the road and other drivers. You had to learn the rules of the road, protocols, and laws. You had to master parallel parking! Now, as a seasoned driver, you hardly give these a moment's thought; they've become automatic. A driver can speed along at 55 miles per hour while having a conversation, listening to a news broadcast, or thinking about work. The body has integrated years of being behind the wheel of a car, so that driving almost seems to do itself; those skills are stored in what's called "implicit memory." The reasons why driving needs to become so immediate, ingrained, habitual, and instinctive are obvious: despite thousands of hours behind the wheel, *every single driving moment happens in the now and must be handled in the present.* If a driver first had to remember and then decide to suddenly brake or change gears, chances are it would be much too late.

My recommendation is to integrate key messaging into daily practice. When this skill is routinely employed as a way to define, address, and communicate, it greatly enhances one's ability to navigate the quickly changing demands of the present. For example, if a meeting is not going well, there can be several reasons, the two most obvious being (1) the subject matter and (2) the dynamics of the participants. The leader who has integrated key messaging into his or her thinking can assess and far more effectively navigate the constantly shifting *whats* of the meeting, both subject matter and personal dynamics.

I've taught the key message template (see below) to leaders in multiple industries the world over. I've instructed country heads in pharmaceuticals from Spain to Turkey, senior bankers from Mexico to Brazil, innovators and tech start-up founders in Silicon Valley, museum curators and advertising executives. Everyone has struggled with it and even resisted it. Why? Because it is hard to do. That said, those who have mastered it have reported back that it is a life-changing technique. It defines problems, ideas, innovations in actionable ways, so that they can be not only communicated effectively but dealt with efficiently. Additionally, key messaging as a problem-solving, management, presentation, and communication tool is highly flexible and can be uniquely tailored for any situation.

These days the majority of presentations are accompanied by a slide deck. If you make time to structure your delivery using key messaging, make sure you do so as well for your slides. (When creating a new presentation, people often refer to previously designed decks, adding or removing individual slides from it. By not starting from scratch, or tailoring the deck to a specific audience, the results are often unclear, haphazard and visually littered.)

Now let's look at the template itself and how to implement it.

THE KEY MESSAGE TEMPLATE

If you search online for an image of a key message template, about a hundred different versions appear. All have value and can be explored. Below is one version of the key message template, where the details, or supporting headlines, of the key messages would be filled in. It is visually uncluttered and very simple. (A blank template that you can use is provided at the end of the chapter.)

Key Messages—Headline Model

Presentation Date:

Presentation Title:

Purpose:

Intended Audience:

KEY MESSAGES
WHAT:
HOW:
WHY:

Headlines		
WHAT: Situation, Idea, Product	**HOW: Actions to Address/Implement**	**WHY: Goals to Aim for/Hoped-for Results**
1.	1.	1.
2.	2.	2.
3.	3.	3.
4.	4.	4.
5.	5.	5.
6.	6.	6.

Purpose and Audience

The first step in designing your key message is to ask yourself what is the purpose of the meeting or exchange. Often people call a meeting, and within just a few minutes, it is abundantly clear that no purpose has been defined. An agenda is not a purpose. The purpose may be to brainstorm, but not having defined that, things can quickly go off the rails. Is the purpose to provide an update? Is it to inform, educate, convince, ask, inspire? Defining the purpose shapes the tone, tenor, and vocabulary of the entire discussion and should be absolutely clear. That is not to say that things cannot digress from a stated purpose. They can. But a clearly defined purpose, combined with well-structured key messages, like a road map, will always bring the discussion or presentation back to the focus of the exchange and get things moving in the right direction.

At the start of designing any key message, you also need to ask yourself about the audience. When using key messaging for presentational purposes, the content should be relevant to the particular audience. So it's crucial to define who the audience members will be, what they already know, and what they'll need to know.

TRY THIS: PURPOSE AND AUDIENCE

To start, take an upcoming work conversation or presentation that you anticipate having in the near future. Then answer these two questions:

Who will the audience be?

What will the purpose be?

Presentation Title

Whether or not you use a title, pushing yourself to think of one is an excellent exercise. Titles set the tone, direction, and parameters of the content. Titles can be witty or have a strongly embedded point of view. By jotting down a few ideas for titles, you will discover a lot about what you need to say and how to say it. Creating a good title is hard, as you'll discover. But it is hard for a reason: it must accomplish a great deal in a few words. Depending on the audience, situation, or corporate culture, titles can be evocative, provocative, rhetorical, interesting, challenging, funny—in essence, not boring. (This is very business-specific, as some companies have very strict rules for titling.) Aim for a title that embeds a word or image that connects to the five senses. For example, a title such as "Fourth Quarter Annual Report" (yawn) can have a subtitle such as "Sailing or Sinking?" That will immediately ignite curiosity in an audience. A mental image of both will be created instantly in the mind of the audience. A well-worded title can capture the whole intention of a presentation and set the direction for the discussion that follows. Even if you wind up not using it, practicing titling is an excellent discipline that enables you to be concise and to the point.

TRY THIS: WHAT'S THE TITLE?

Take three or four recent business events or challenges and give each two or three different titles, each of which should take into consideration both your point of view and the audience.

What did you learn by doing that?

Key Messages

All key messages need to answer three questions:

Key Messages

- **WHAT:** The *what* can be a key concept, situation, innovation, challenge. It is the single overarching element and should be described in under ten words.
- **HOW:** The *how* refers to the actions to address or implement the above. One main action is recommended, also to be described in very few words.
- **WHY:** The *why* focuses on the desired outcomes; these are goals to aim for, the hoped-for results. List the single most important result in as few words as possible.

Headlines

Headlines further develop and define specific aspects of the situation, key action, and main hoped-for result. The headlines can and would change depending on the purpose of the exchange, as you will see from some examples filled in below. Strong headlines set and guide the agenda, illuminate your key messages, and generate questions and responses from the audience. The examples below are a guide. Keep in mind that the more you begin to employ key messaging, the more you'll be able to tweak it and make it valuable for your purposes.

What a Key Message Might Look Like

Here are a few samples of how the template might be designed depending on different audiences and goals regarding a burning building.

- Presentation Title: Everyone Is Safe (versus, for example, "Raging Fire Puts Lives at Risk!" Note the difference.)
- Date:
- Purpose: Update
- Intended Audience: General population

Key Messages

- **WHAT:** Burning occupied property

- **HOW:** Call fire department
- **WHY:** Save lives

Headlines		
WHAT	**HOW**	**WHY**
Occupied property	Call fire department	Save lives
6 elderly occupants	Evacuate people	Save property
3 children	Call neighbors	Prevent spread
Large building nearby	Call ambulance	
10 stories	Alert local hospital	
100-year-old building	Seek volunteers	

One of the benefits of this design tool is its flexibility. For example, if this presentation is to the firefighting crew, the *whats*, and thus the *hows* and *whys*, might be entirely different.

WHAT	**HOW**	**WHY**
Asbestos	Supply needed escape harness	Crew safety
Wooden structure	Secure extra breathing aparatus	
Low water pressure	Provide heat resistant hoods	
High winds	Set up barriors	

The firefighter audience for this message needs to know wholly different things than does the media or the public at large. *Tailoring the message to the given audience is critical to make connection work.* As you can see, the headlines, which deepen and develop the content, are completely different in these two examples. Why? Because of the different audiences and purposes.

Also the flexibility of this design allows the presentation to drill down into any of the specific *whats* or *hows* in as much detail as required. The *what* of asbestos could have its own key messages:

Headline: Asbestos		
WHAT	**HOW**	**WHY**
Chrysotile	Personal Alert Safety System	Limit exposure
Popcorn ceiling	SCBA respirator	Containment
Drywall	Decontaminate	
Floor tiles		
Basement location		

Here is another example, and a not infrequent one in business:

- **WHAT:** Competitor's product launch will cut our market share
- **HOW:** Speed up timelines for our product rollout
- **WHY:** Beat the competition

WHAT	**HOW**	**WHY**
Our product is at risk	Increase budget to move up advertising	Stay ahead of competition
Rollout date is behind competition	Identify other bottlenecks in rollout plan	Increase product visibility
Launch date delayed by marketing and advertising inefficiencies	Add to headcount to move up launch date	Keep current clients
Insufficient staff to address	Increase competitive intelligence	Gain new business
	Do targeted rollout to speed up timeline	

Any of the above *whats* can be described in much greater detail than the chart provides. The chart serves as a guide that sets the direction and organizes how the information will be delivered. So, for example, advertising inefficiencies might be due to any number of factors: workload, indecision, budget, regulatory approvals. That particular *what* could be given its own template as a way to take a deep dive into the reasons behind the delay. Following that, its own set of actions could then be established.

TRY THIS: DETAIL THE KEY MESSAGES

After filling in the title, purpose, audience, and three main overall key messages, drill down into the specific aspects of the *what* (situation, idea, innovation, or challenge) that elaborates or builds on the big key message (see "The Key Message Template"). Those are your headlines. List each as it occurs to you in random order, without prioritizing or explaining. If, during list making, ideas of how to address any of those aspects arise, jot them in the "How" (actions to address) column. The *whats* and *hows* do not need to apply to each other. Each column is its own separate unit. (When this message is delivered through either a conversation or a formal presentation, each column should be presented separately, as the audience will be better able to track the information as opposed to constantly tracking back and forth between *whats*, *hows*, and *whys*.) Finally, list the hoped-for results, or *whys*. Put the list away and come back to it in an hour to review, prioritize, or delete items that may not be necessary. In other words, edit it. Why prioritize? Two reasons: First, prioritizing will identify where to place emphasis on key points that will receive the most time. Second, due to time constraints, meetings or presentations are often cut short, and if the most critical content isn't delivered first, it may not be delivered at all.

METAPHORS AND SIMILES

Why do we use metaphors and similes? What purpose do they serve? We are connected to our surroundings by our five senses, and metaphors are the linguistic equivalent of providing someone a map when in a foreign city. The last sentence was a metaphor. It provided an imaginary picture and sensory recall. Metaphors trigger an emotional response in the brain. Metaphors allow us to feel and respond at a sense level to ideas or concepts. They bridge the gap (there's one!) between the idea and the body. They litter (there's another!) our speech. They hit the mark or leave us in the dark. (Two more!) The previous three are rather standard issue, and not terribly original. Better to attempt something a bit more creative and less hackneyed. Why use them? Because they work! And if the goal as a communicator is to connect with your audience, metaphors provide the emotional glue. Using the situation or idea that was key-messaged above, consider which metaphors might adequately capture it. To what is the situation similar or analogous? Search for metaphors that aren't commonplace, but descriptive.

TRY THIS: METAPHOR/SIMILE PRACTICE

Attempt to find three or four metaphors or similes (which use the word *like* or *as* to compare two ideas) for each of the listed subjects below and see how they tilt the point of view or subtextual feeling regarding the subject:

Traveling these days is _____

A new product launch is like _____

Meeting with my boss is like _____

Managing office politics is as difficult as _____

A job interview is _____

Public speaking is _____

PowerPoint is like _____

PRIMING

In an article in *Journal of Experimental Psychology: Learning, Memory, and Cognition,* Larry Jacoby writes: "Priming refers to an increased sensitivity to certain stimuli due to prior experience. Because priming is believed to occur outside of conscious awareness, it is different from memory, which relies on the direct retrieval of information. Direct retrieval utilizes explicit memory, while priming relies on implicit memory. Research has also shown that the effects of priming can impact the decision-making process." In *Psychology Today,* priming is defined as follows: "Priming is a nonconscious form of human memory concerned with perceptual identification of words and objects. It refers to activating particular representations or associations in memory just before carrying out an action or task. For example, a person who sees the word 'yellow' will be slightly faster to recognize the word 'banana.' This happens because yellow and banana are closely associated in memory. Additionally, priming can also refer to a technique in psychology used to train a person's memory in both positive and negative ways."

Regarding presenting, priming is critical, because once that sensitivity has been created, the listener's mind will be waiting for whatever was primed to be further enhanced. So in a communication, for example, imagine the metaphor "We'll be on thin ice if" followed by "we meet with this customer," "buy this property," "don't follow these regulations." The listener's mind will have instantly, and unconsciously, created an image of walking gingerly on ice or even falling into freezing water. That prime will set up a quiet alarm, or inner stress, in the listener. That may very well suit the message and do precisely what is needed. However, if that is not the goal, it would be best to choose a less worrying metaphor. Metaphors and priming are powerful. The famous "Don't think of elephants" is a perfect example, as the animals are conjured with the word before you even have a chance to resist.

Here is a very basic example of priming: Let's say a communication is introduced with the words, "There are three critical issues to discuss," but then only two are covered. In that case, the listener's brain will have been primed for three issues, will be expecting three issues, and will be distracted, perhaps even unconsciously disappointed, if the third is not delivered. Or conversely, if the brain is primed for three and *four* are delivered, the fourth might be missed entirely, as the brain might have either tuned out or felt misled. In other words, to make sure connection happens—that the thoughts, ideas, suggestions, feelings from the speaker easily leap into the audience members' minds—priming should be used appropriately, judiciously, and carefully.

No matter what the purpose of any communication may be, at root it must be supported by the speaker's conviction. Data can be compelling, and often it is vital information that must be conveyed. But data alone will not sway or move an audience. Imagine Hamlet's famous "To be or not to be" soliloquy delivered as just raw data, mere lists of words. No one would care; no one would listen. It is the emotional quest beneath the words—the confusion, fear, and ambivalence with which the actor infuses the language—that moves an audience. Often clients say, "But in business the data is all-important; it is what an audience expects." There is no discounting the value of accumulated information. But data can be put on a chart! Data does not need a voice. But communication does. It needs *you*, and to be effective, data needs to be driven by what you *think, know, and feel*. Just as Hamlet's speech needs to be infused with varying emotions, data needs to be infused with your suggestions, advocacy, gut sense of what's right or wrong, your passion. Passion does not need to be overly emphasized. Yelling, overtalking, wild gestures, over-the-top emotions are not passion. (That's overacting, or as is said in the theater, "chewing the scenery!") Passion is conviction. Conviction combined with knowledge has the power to sway an audience.

A CEO with whom I work admits proudly, "I surround myself with people who are smarter than I am. I listen to them, weigh their expert opinion, and make my decisions." His decision-making process is a soup of raw data combined with knowledge, expertise, and gut sense upon which he relies. For him, his advisors' feelings hold as much weight as the data. Why? Because they are feelings informed by history and knowledge. No one can know the future, but predictions can be made based upon past experience. Brains, as pattern seekers, predict outcomes based on previously experienced patterns. That happens on the most basic physical level. If you've ever taken one extra step up or down on a stairway that wasn't actually there, you know exactly what I mean. The brain established the distance that the foot automatically needed to go, and whoops, no step! It's a shocking feeling, but it describes exactly what prediction is. We do the same with other kinds of information, or attempt to, all the time. You can predict the word at the end of this . . . That's an easy one! But since we predict so automatically and unconsciously, it's vital as communicators and presenters that we have a comprehensive understanding of how design, as well as delivery, can move or impact an audience. Organization, key messaging, metaphors, priming, passion, and prediction—all these are tools that enable the raw data of content to be shaped into meaningful and effective exchanges *between* people. Key messaging provides an architectural story form. That is another great reason why the structure is so effective, as it follows an organic story format.

The last step when designing a communication for presentational purposes is to return to the needs of the audience. Once the key messages have been established, it's important to anticipate what questions a particular audience may have. Write down those questions and your answers. Return to the presentation and embed any information that the imagined questions brought to light.

The aim of all of the above exercises is to enable communication that is clearly designed, purpose-driven, and audience relevant. Practicing key messaging so that it becomes second nature will increase your ability to navigate complex people dynamics, as well as challenging business imperatives. One client discovered that by having all the people on his team key-message ideas or problems together, they came up with far better solutions. (His boss noticed so much improvement with the team that he too asked to be taught the system.) Because the model can be either very detailed, with long lists of *whats* or *hows*, or extremely lean, with just one key message for each category, it can be employed both for deep dives with peers and experts and for high-level executive summaries. The architecture will support either detailed or streamlined approaches. See the following example using the human body systems:

- WHAT: Human body systems
- HOW: Each system works
- WHY: To support life

WHAT	HOW	WHY
Respiratory system	Breathe	Transfer oxygen, remove Co2
Digestive system	Eat	Convert food into energy
Nervous system	Feel	Transmit electical signals throughout body
Circulatory system	Heart/lungs pump/ breathe	Transport nutrients/oxygen to cells

Now drill down into the digestive system with its specific list of *whats*, *hows*, and *whys*.

- **WHAT:** Human body systems: digestive
- **HOW:** Each system works: absorb nutrients
- **WHY:** To support life: provide energy

WHAT	HOW	WHY
Mouth	Chewing	Gross breakdown
Esophagus	Enzymes	Conversion of calories to energy
Stomach	Acids	
Large intestines		

WHY DRIVER

Sometimes the goal of a communication is to influence rather than inform. In those situations, begin with the *why* instead of the *what*. This is most critical when the *why* is aligned with the audience's values and aspirations. Returning to the analogy of the physician, is the *why* to heal a sick patient or merely to reduce pain? In business, is the *why* to make a profit, to provide customer satisfaction, or to be socially responsible? (It can be all three, but which is the driver for which audience? Which might inspire action?) A communication that is driven by values or intent places the purpose at the beginning and can persuade an audience precisely because it is so candid. Always know the purpose of the exchange so you can design it accordingly.

BEGINNING, MIDDLE, AND END

Finally, the beauty of key messaging is that its architecture is story-driven, and stories are our glue. Stories are how we describe our world to each other. They allow us to understand events, ideas, and people beyond our immediate experience. They engage our emotions and imagination.

Think of your business innovation, idea, problem, or solution as a character in a journey. Many novel ideas face fierce resistance. Galileo's notion that the earth circled the sun, so radical for its time, took hundreds of years to become accepted reality. If your idea is ahead of its time or conflicts with your organization's culture, it may clash with management's expectations. How can you express an idea in a way that changes your audience's mind? Don't shy away from the conflict. Explore it. In his classic book *The Hero with a Thousand Faces*, Joseph Campbell describes the arc of the mythological hero: "A hero ventures forth from the world of common day into a region of supernatural wonder: fabulous forces are there encountered and a decisive victory is won. The hero comes back from this mysterious adventure with the power to bestow boons on his fellow man."

Heros venture into new territories, navigate obstacles, and overcome them. So too must novel business ideas. Describe the current circumstance, detail how your idea will address that given challenge, dig into the potential conflicts, and unpack the ways your idea will overcome those obstacles to arrive at, it is hoped, its flourishing. The architecture of myth and the hero's journey have been around for thousands of years for a good reason: they work! They move hearts *and* minds. Give them a shot.

A journalist with whom I've worked told me he spends more time on crafting his lead, the first sentence of a story, than almost anything else. He knows that that single sentence alone will determine whether or not the reader continues reading. Granted, everyone is motivated by personal interest, but think back to a surprising story you fully committed time to reading because of a captivating headline or lead. Capture your audience's attention with a powerful lead; use the key message template to design the message; think of how you might use the hero's journey to craft the story of your idea. Priming, metaphors, vibrant vocabulary, point of view, these will carry your audience through the story to your conclusion. Never forget that architecture is essential and that story structure is in our social DNA.

Chapter 7: Designing Messages to Increase Presence

Review Exercises

- **Purpose and Audience**—identify intention of exchange and who will receive it
- **What's the Title?**—frame the content in a way that elicits a strong response, embeds your point of view
- **Detail the Key Messages**—design impactful, clear, concise delivery of content
- **Metaphor/Simile Practice**—find images to create parallel ways of explaining content

Exercise Name	Frequency Goal / Actual	Observations	Next Steps
Key Meassage	When have upcoming deliverable	Made content delivery much clearer	Employ for meetings
	/		
	/		
	/		
	/		

Key Messages—Headline Model

Presentation Date:

Presentation Title:

Purpose:

Intended Audience:

KEY MESSAGES

WHAT is the situation (concept, problem, idea, challenge):

HOW can you address it (recommended actions):

WHY (goals, results, desired outcome):

Headlines		
WHAT: Situation	**HOW: Actions**	**WHY: Results**
1.	1.	1.
2.	2.	2.
3.	3.	3.
4.	4.	4.
5.	5.	5.
6.	6.	6.

Presentation or Conversation? The Style of Delivery

"Make sure you have finished speaking before your audience has finished listening."

—Dorothy Sarnoff

One aspect of presence is the ability to fluidly move between the varied "yous" with ease. The overly used word *authentic*—as in "authentic leadership," be your "authentic self"—is really a misnomer, because in truth there is no single "authentic" you. If there is, which is it? Is it the one who promises, indeed *swears*, to get up at 5:30 a.m. and go to the gym, or the one who, when the alarm goes off, pushes the snooze button and sleeps for another hour? Both are you. Both are the true "authentic" you. Certainly, regarding such things as currency and pharmaceuticals, authentic versus bogus is vital and clear, but when it comes to people, we enter entirely different realms of complexity. Every one of us consists of multiple selves. Each person has several styles, countless communicative talents and deficiencies that become manifest in constantly shifting situations.

If we eliminate the word *presentation*, as I recommend, and replace it with *conversation*, when you do "present," what kind of conversation do you want

171

to have? Which style of you is being called upon to communicate: the formal, relaxed, challenging, inspirational, urgent? The appropriate style depends upon several things: the audience, the situation, the purpose, and the content. We don't explain complex concepts to five-year-olds the way we do to subject experts. We organically know how to tailor our delivery, approach, vocabulary, and tone to suit the needs of our audience. That's not being inauthentic; it's understanding that to connect we must have *diverse styles of delivery*.

Many clients have asked me, "But how can I know what the audience expectations are?" You can't always. But you can know your objectives, and those will, in part, determine your style of delivery. And given the situation, you can pretty much grasp what the audience will be hoping for as well. The types of questions that I'm typically asked are too numerous to list. Here's a brief sample: "How should I dress?" "What if I get thirsty?" "I usually pace and like to walk around. Is that OK?" "Should I stand behind or beside the podium?" "Can I hold the podium?" "Can I have notes?" "Should I memorize or just know my bullets?"

The answer to each is quite specific, but for general purposes, I offer three simple words: *do your research*.

PPPPP: PRIOR PLANNING PREVENTS POOR PERFORMANCE

Investigate. Whenever possible, get into the space where you will be having your "conversation" well ahead of time to see what it feels and looks like. If you'll be in a boardroom or conference room, find out what the seating arrangement will be. I recently coached a group of senior executives for board and trustee presentations. It was a large national organization, with many trustees on the elderly side, and the speakers told me that at times it's been a challenge to keep the trustees awake. I asked to see the boardroom. It was a huge windowless room, beige, with wall-to-wall carpeting and padded fabric walls! No wonder people slip off to the land of nod; it was like walking into a nursery! But having seen the room and discovered its muffled acoustics, we spent the next three days redesigning everyone's presentations to make them dynamic, brief, targeted, and fun. We found ways to get the board members to stay engaged by having the presenters ask questions; we practiced ways that presenters could move around the space and not be stuck behind the podium; we replaced data with stories; we used novel images and fun visuals to liven up the decks; we shortened the presentations and made time for dialogue, and we used the key message struc-ture. In short, we adapted and adjusted. It was the first time in recent memory that no one slept!

TRY THIS: BE PREPARED

Make your list of questions. Here are some ideas to get you started on your research. Is there a stage? A podium? Will people be behind desks or not? If there will be a slide presentation, where will the projector be? What equipment will be provided? Will any technology be used, and if so, what is it? Where will you need to stand so that you are not moving in front of the light source and creating a shadow? Will you deliver seated or standing? If you need to advance your slides, is there a remote or clicker? If not, how will you advance the slides? Will water be available, and if so, in what sort of container? What are the acoustics of the room like? Is the sound bright and crisp or muffled and flat?

These may all seem like tiny details, but as they say, the devil is in the details. How many times have you sat through a presentation, unable to see a section of a slide because the speaker was blocking it or casting a shadow over it? As a speaker, you want as much as is possible to be in the driver's seat, and the first step is to know what you'll be driving.

Jewelry that jingles, earrings that dangle and collide with a head mike, bangs that hide your eyes, hair that falls into your face, glasses that slip down your nose, clothes that are uncomfortable—there are countless distractors that can pull your and your audience's focus as well as impact your comfort and credi-bility. Only by knowing everything you can ahead of time about all the physical factors of both yourself and the space can you hope to have some mastery over how you will, as they say in the theater, "take stage." (Keep in mind that you are "taking stage" from the moment you leave your seat until you arrive at the spot where you'll deliver. How you walk to that space, how you stand once you get there, how you look around and connect—all will be observed.)

The first 15 to 30 seconds of any delivery need to be very well practiced. Adrenalin usually floods the body, so it's crucial to rehearse so as to address that chemical shift. My chief recommendation is to have the opening of your text so thoroughly embedded in mind and body that no matter what happens, it can be delivered without even thinking. Those first few seconds can really feel like an out-of-body experience. If you have your opening two or three sentences down cold, as in you-could-say-them-in-your-sleep solid, they'll roll off your tongue with no thought, giving you the time to adjust to the room, the audience, and your own metabolic shift. During those first few moments, the audience also needs time to get used to you, your style, tone, pace, accent, voice, appearance, and gestures. That first half-minute is a mini-duet of all parties feeling each other out. After a minute or so, speakers tend to relax and find their stride, the body calms down, and tension recedes. Then the fun can begin!

TRY THIS: DOWN COLD

Memorize the opening two to three sentences of your talk. Sing them. Say them 20 times as rapidly as you possibly can. Say them in your mind as you walk down the street. Say them when you wake up and right before you go to sleep. Turn on the radio and say them while the radio plays. Do not memorize the tone, emphasis, inflection—just the words.

Each delivery style needs to be tailored to the content, context, and goals of the event. Some must be more formal, others relaxed. At TED, for example, the standard rule for men is no ties (though some have refused to obey!). It's a high-stakes presentation in a relaxed atmosphere.

One of my clients, an advertising agency, had made pitches through several levels of a large, urban institution. The presenters had a final one to give, to the chairman of the board. "Have you Googled him?" I asked. They hadn't. We looked at the chairman's bio, and I insisted that for this final pitch, they all had to wear ties. "We never wear ties. Ever," one pushed back. "You will tomorrow," I insisted. "This is a very conservative man from another generation, who will immediately note your sartorial choices." They wore ties; they got the client. Would they have anyway? Quite possibly. But by briefly shifting their style to align more closely with that of the prospective client, they removed one potential hurdle. (A banker client who is a serious watch collector told me how careful he is when selecting which watch to wear for a given client: Rolex for his business deals in Switzerland, Timex for those in Ohio, and never the reverse. I think of this as situational presence, shifting one's style to suit the situation.)

TRY THIS: STYLE SELECTION

I recommend getting answers to as many of the following questions as possible ahead of time to help determine your delivery style: Why are you the designated presenter? Is it your knowledge, role, reputation, relationship? What is the style and tenor of the event? Even if you are a speaker who is introducing someone else, why have you been selected to do so? How can that small detail shape your remarks? Answering these questions will help you prepare your presentation:

- What is the main story you wish to tell?
- What are the three *most* important points you want your listeners to remember?
- If you could deliver only *one* critical message, what would it be? Why?
- Return to key messaging: What is the purpose and/or business imperative of the meeting or discussion?
- Who is the intended audience, and what are the audience's expectations?
- Who else might or will be present?
- Is the audience specific or general? Casual or formal?
- What will the members of the audience know already?

- What will they want or need to know in addition to that?
- Was a detailed preread or backup deck sent to the audience members? Will they have read it and want it addressed?
- Is interaction expected? If so, will this be an audience receptive to open-ended questions? What questions might the audience have?
- Is there a distinct time for Q&A?
- Will people be participating virtually? If so, how?
- Are there other speakers?
  - What is the order of the speakers?
  - What time will you be speaking?
  - How long are you expected to speak?
- Is there a theme that you need to weave into your content?
- Is there a dress code?
- Will the event be video-recorded? And if so, what is the best attire for that? (No stripes!)
- What is your close? Will it be a call to action? A summary? A quote?

Anything that can be found out and answered ahead of time should be considered. Based on your previous experiences, it's highly recommended to customize your own list of questions, so that you can get the answers beforehand.

Once you've written your text, it is essential to read it out loud. Words on paper have a very different ring and sound than spoken words. Do the words flow? Are they easy to pronounce? Do they feel right in the mouth? Is the vocabulary appropriate for the given situation and audience? Read it, edit it, and reread it aloud. This process may require several iterations, but each draft should get you closer to the final copy.

HOW TO REHEARSE

Once you have your final draft, read it aloud while seated and then do so while standing. Notice if, while on your feet, you move randomly. Put newspaper under your feet. If you shift your weight or unconsciously step backward and forward, the newspaper will crunch. That's a good indication you may be moving from nerves and without intention. As you speak aloud, notice the places in the text where you'd like to put greater emphasis. Mark those places in the script. Underline them or use a highlighter. Note language that is not crystal clear or where it's overwritten or repetitive. Words said aloud have a very different impact than those read off a page. They are embodied and as a result have much greater "sticking power." Revise your text so it is as clear and concise as possible. Imagine a question, and answer it. Practice, practice, practice. The best communicators became the best from practice!

After you've rehearsed by yourself, it can be very helpful to gather a small audience of colleagues or friends to watch your talk *ahead of time*. If you decide to have a practice audience, make sure to discuss beforehand the goals of the rehearsal itself. Will the audience give you feedback on the content, clarity, and organization? On your delivery style? Are the people in your audience there to role-play Q&A? Are they there to watch or listen for any physical or vocal habits you are trying to correct? Rehearsals can serve multiple purposes, but are most helpful when the goals are clearly stated *in advance by you, the speaker*. Also, the format for providing feedback should be established at the beginning. One helpful structure is called *observation-impact-suggestion*. For example, with observation: "I noticed you looked at the floor a lot." Impact: "It made me wonder if you had forgotten your text." Suggestion: "Try making eye contact with us with your focus shifting to a few different people around the room." Here's another example: Observation: "I noticed you turned your back to us a lot so that you could see the screen behind you." Impact: "I couldn't hear you when you turned away." Suggestion: "Try glancing at your notes or a computer in front of you so you aren't turning away so much."

Concerning audience feedback, it's essential to request that the language used be clear and supportive and deliver *actionable* suggestions. Insensitively worded critiques can really devastate a speaker, especially a nervous one! As the speaker, make sure that you establish the feedback guidelines so as to help and not hinder your confidence. If someone delivers a critique that only makes you feel worse, ask for suggestions that can help to remediate what the person observed. If the person doesn't know how to fix the problem, then ask him or her to reword the feedback in a way that can be actionable or incorporated on your end. Observe the difference: "You look like a nervous wreck pacing all over the place" versus "Moving around is OK, especially for a reason. Stillness has a lot of power too. See if you can find moments to be still." The slightest difference in the delivery of a critique can have significant impact. As the person requesting a rehearsal audience, make sure that you set very clear expectations for feedback.

TRY THIS: OBSERVATION-IMPACT-SUGGESTION

Before a practice rehearsal with friends or colleagues, teach them "Observation-Impact-Suggestion" and do a trial run before delivering your talk to make sure everyone understands the practice.

While onstage, actors can see what's going on backstage, but no matter what they see, they have to stay *inside* the world of the play. While delivering a consistent performance, they also have to make night-by-night, moment-by-moment adjustments to suit the particulars of each audience. Beyond being aware of their own performance, they also need to be sensitive to the small adjustments their fellow actors are making. In other words, there are multiple levels of observation and reaction going on simultaneously. This may sound impossible, but it's one of the most thrilling aspects of live performance. Every sense is heightened, alert, connected.

When speaking publicly, the same degree of focus, along with instant adjustments, is required. To connect with an audience, you have to take the audience members in, not shut them out. To communicate effectively, you have to be keenly aware of all the signals coming your way and adjust accordingly. On the other hand, it is very important not to project onto the audience what you *think* may be going on. Once, when I was teaching a course in presentation skills, my video camera stopped working in the middle of someone's presentation. I was worried about not capturing the footage but didn't want to inter-rupt the speaker. Without my realizing it, I began to frown. The speaker, having noticed me frowning but not knowing why, assumed I was angry at him. This completely threw him. His focus was split between his speech and his worry over my presumed "anger." He lost his train of thought, and it took him time to regain his composure. (This was all revealed during the postdelivery critique.)

That said, there is a very delicate balance between acutely observing the signals coming at you from the audience and accurately assessing them in the moment. Try not to assume or project upon flat facial expressions. Some people listen with very blank expressions; others with very reactive faces. Some listen by staring at the ceiling, or closing their eyes. On the other hand, if you feel as though you are not connecting, pause. Briefly. Take a breath; make eye contact; vary your vocal pace and energy. Do whatever possible to bring yourself back to yourself and bring along others who are with you. Again, remember, most fre-quently it is tension that blocks connection. Whatever you can do to relax and remove whatever is preventing the connection will only increase your bond with the audience.

IT'S NOT PERSONAL

Often when clients have to give a speech or present to senior management, they're extremely worried about how they'll come across, if they'll get a question they can't answer, if their request will be rejected or their suggestions ignored, contradicted, or even belittled. They become consumed with anxiety. I pose a hypothetical situation: "If I come to your house and you offer me a bowl of fruit and I decline it, I even say I don't like fruit, am I rejecting you or the fruit?"

"The fruit," they say.

"Is it possible in your role at work to think the same way? Imagine you are bringing senior management some fruit; if they reject it—as in they do not take your idea—is that a rejection of *you* or your *idea?*"

"But the idea is *mine! I thought it up.*"

"Really?" I ask. "Is any idea really *yours?*"

It really makes waves when I question this notion of "ownership." Everything we know has been learned, borrowed, and built upon. Yes, we have ideas all the time, but the fierce attachment to *this is "my" idea* feels a lot to me like a three-year-old refusing to share. Our ideas, intelligence, original creations all exist on a continuum and exist in relation to what has come before and will come well after us. (A great book, *E=mc²: The Biography of a Formula* by David Bodanis, explores how even Einstein's brilliant and astonishing discovery grew out of a continuum of insights going back 200 years! A great read, which I highly recommend.) When we identify with and insist upon sole ownership of our ideas, their rejection feels both personal and painful. But if our ideas are there to serve the greater good, are offered and then let go, the impact will be far different. If they are not about proving how smart, talented, and brilliant we are, we need not attach so fiercely to the reactions they get, whether *positive or negative*. Here is a fun, and some may argue wacky, way to conceptualize ideas: The idea borrowed *your* brain, used *your* voice, body, and communication skills as a medium of *its* expression. You were merely the agent, not the owner. This is a really hard one for most people to accept. We take pride in "our" intelligence, "our" advanced degrees, "our" acquired job titles. But consequently we feel terribly hurt or offended when "our" ideas are ignored or rejected, when "our" project is not approved. We personalize things, get all worked up, ruminate, become consumed by jealousy, depression, even rage.

Here the seeds of office politics take root. When egos take over, going to work becomes akin to doing battle. Conversely, when ideas, suggestions, and opinions are conceptualized as something being offered, that bowl of fruit again, and if indeed the fruit is rejected, ignored, or worse insulted, it is not *you* who is wrong or stupid or ignored. You are not the banana! That you are not the banana is clear as day to anyone. But when we merge with and insist upon ego ownership of what we offer, that's when things become personal. That you are not your ideas is quite hard for most to grasp and accept, but definitely worth aiming for. It may sound somewhat utopian and even foolish, given how most of the world operates. Nonetheless I offer it as a concept to explore as a way to counteract taking things so personally. Many clients have reported that saying "I am not the banana" to themselves before a high-stakes presentation has not only relaxed them but turned fear into funny.

HANDLING Q&A: CURIOSITY OR CONFLICT

A client recently defined the culture of her organizations as a "gotcha" culture, meaning that questions asked following, or even interrupting, a presentation were meant to prove either how smart the questioner was or how misguided the speaker was. In other words, questions were not posed for clarification or new information but as a power play. Aggressive questions make everyone uneasy. If not held in check, that style can spread like the flu through an organization, making everyone vulnerable. Whenever possible, it is best to defuse that kind of behavior with active listening.

The term *active listening* has been in general use for some time. It requires that when asked a question, you don't automatically begin to think of your answer before you've fully understood the core ask. You wait until the key concept of the question has been stated. Often questioners will ramble or cover a number of challenges before they get to the point. While listening, the speaker will begin to process-listen, or frame the response, and will no longer be actively listening to the questioner. After a prelude a questioner will usually have a turn word or phrase—*why, when, what, where, how much, what if*—followed by the core question. Wait for that turn word or phrase and listen acutely to what follows and then repeat the precise words at the very top of your answer. I repeat, say the precise words of the questioner at the beginning of your reply. What this does is tell the questioner, "I hear *you*, not my agenda." It also repeats the question for those who may not have heard it, a great time-saver. There is no need to repeat the entire question. That can become quite tiresome. Just echo back the core. With aggressive questioning, active listening buys you time, as you repeat the core words, to gather your thoughts and frame your response. (Usually people buy time with pat statements such as "That's a great question" or "Thanks for asking that.") Repeating the precise core words honors the question, defuses defensiveness, and puts you on equal footing with the questioner.

Again, due to the stress of Q&A and aggressive questions, it's only natural for listening well to go out the window.

TRY THIS: PRACTICE REHEARSAL FOR EFFECTIVE Q&A WITH ACTIVE LISTENING

Active listening is an art and needs to be practiced. If you do a practice rehearsal, make sure you add that to your process. Ask your audience to ask questions, so that you can practice answering actively.

PREPLANNING VERSUS WRITING THE SCRIPT

Given that we are such excellent predictors, we often find ourselves "writing the script" before we've even encountered the situation. It's a common outcome of working in a highly competitive or aggressive culture. What do I mean by that? Think of the number of times you've negatively imagined how a conversation will go, working yourself into a bit of a tizzy before you've had the conversation in reality. I'm differentiating that from positively imagining an outcome—as in the "Standing O" exercise in Chapter 1, which can be great practice when prepping for a challenging delivery. Also it differs from attempting to determine anticipatory or challenging questions. That's called preplanning. "Writing the script," as I define it, is different. It is essentially driven by anxiety or defensiveness and sets up an unconscious, imaginary antagonism.

For example, to get cast in a play, actors have to audition. Actors can imagine the outcome any number of ways. But often due to their needing work, or their vulnerability, they will imagine themselves at the "mercy" of an all-powerful director who will or won't "allow" them to work. This imaginary script sets off a level of fear and subtle antagonism that can be sensed by a director, and it's an automatic turnoff. A director has a short amount of time, a tight budget, and a massive amount to pull together before opening night. The director is looking for someone to *solve* problems, not to make more of them! Every director wants an actor to enter the audition room fully confident that he or she can serve the role, solve problems, and be a team player.

Is any job interview any different? Is any negotiation any different? Is any presentation followed by aggressive Q&A with senior management any different? All parties in these situations are looking for solutions, not problems. And yet! How often we "write a negative script" and turn the director, headhunter, boss, interviewer, audience, or questioner into an adversary. I used to tell my acting students that an audition is not about getting a job. That can and does happen, but perhaps for only 1 out of 50 or more auditions. To make those other 49 worthwhile, the actor needs to write another—positive—script, to look at auditioning as an opportunity to deliver any number of options: to meet new creative people, to make bold unexpected acting choices, to practice craft, to try a new point of view and frameshift, to focus out and assess the director for his or her style, to audition the room from the actor's point of view, to be curious. The actor should strive to approach auditioning not as a desperate attempt to get a job but as *inquiry*, as that radically changes the experience. These exact same shifts in perspectives can be brought to a myriad of stressful business situations. In terms of style, its worthwhile to become aware of habitual negative scripts you write that may impact how you are perceived is worthwhile.

Additionally, when we come into a situation having "decided" the bottom line, or having "written" the script beforehand, we miss or ignore vast amounts of information *in the present*. The tunnel vision that results eliminates our ability to perceive opportunities that relaxed curiosity can reveal. If the stakes are high and fight or flight kicks in, the ability to manage that response with wonder and curiosity is powerful. Indeed, to be curious about one's counterpart in any high-stakes conversation, negotiation, Q&A, or conflict is one of the most effective ways to connect. To be curious immediately changes the dynamic and creates avenues for unanticipated exchange, connection, and communication. We know so little about one another; by boxing ourselves in and "writing the script" ahead of time, we leave very little wiggle room for finding alternatives. Curiosity is about being open to another's reality without assuming you know anything. It is magic. And for a "gotcha" culture, it is the best way to avoid feeling "caught."

OPEN-ENDED SCRIPT

What language might be used to defuse the stress of any of the contexts described above: interviews, negotiations, aggressive Q&A after a delivery? Consider the appropriate style and the objectives of the exchange. Vocabulary can have a huge impact on the outcome of any exchange. Seek words that are inclusive and respectful and that engender the free flow of ideas rather than stubborn insistence. To counter aggression or challenges with curiosity requires practice and forethought.

TRY THIS: KEEP THE CONVERSATION GOING

Write a list of aggressive, challenging, or even borderline insulting questions or remarks. Take some time and write answers or responses that address those remarks in a way that won't add fuel to the fire or seem defensive, but will encourage a deeper exploration of the subject. See how using such phrasing as "From your perspective, how might," "I'm curious; what if we look at it like this," "If I understand you correctly," "What I'm hearing is," "Might we consider?" Seek language and phrasing that don't take the bait of the aggression, but also keep unpacking the differing opinions in a way that yields collaboration instead of combat.

If you use the key message template as a way to design a presentation deck, the acts of designing, editing, and structuring will only increase your familiarity with and grasp of the material you'll be delivering. In that case, memorization won't be necessary. Sometimes questions are asked during a presentation that require an answer well ahead of where you are in your delivery. The template, which allows for very clear and lean slides, will, like a road map, easily take you back to where you were. When you do catch up to the slide for which you've already answered the question, you'll see that you've covered that material and can skip past it or very briefly reiterate as needed.

Regarding slide design itself, I always recommend simple and uncluttered slides. The simple reason is *people cannot read and listen at the same time.* If detailed or highly complex material needs to be delivered, it can be sent ahead as an advance preread presentation to those who will be in attendance. That way, audience members can give proper time, thought, and attention to what you will be delivering, which will be more of an "executive" summary. What do I mean by uncluttered? Lots of white space, crisp visuals, consistent fonts, bulleted items of five to seven words maximum so that the audience can quickly glance and grab the information without having to read. Less is more.

When delivering, the presentation deck will be ancillary to the detailed preread presentation document. The structure for the presentation deck should follow the key message template. The first slide would have your title with subtitle, name, and date. Before you delve into the content and while the title slide is up, introduce your metaphor or thematically related anecdote. Slide two would have your three key messages: situation (burning building); action (call fire department), result (prevent spread). They should be stated and *not explained.* What this does is prime the audience for the three most critical aspects of what you will discuss: your main *what,* your greatest recommended action to address that *what,* and your most significant hoped-for result. You are also telling the audience right at the beginning what your reason is for your recommended actions. Slide three would detail the situation, the *what.* It would list in bullet form the critical aspects of the situation for that given audience. For example, it would describe the relevant and prioritized aspects of the burning building. Four to five bulleted items of five to seven words should suffice. These are your talking points and are on the slide to allow the audience to quickly grab the key concepts visually while listening to you explain the situation in detail. Slide four would then state the actions, the *hows,* to address the burning building. Slide five, the reasons *why.* The last slide could be next steps or a call to action. I've found that a summary is not necessary when the content is so clearly laid out. This design can even be delivered on a single slide as a guideline for conversation.

Whatever design you choose to implement, designing well ahead of time for a given audience becomes a kind of mental rehearsal. It is essential to speak it out loud to craft transitional language between the slides and to see if what you've created flows logically. Remember to practice and choose a style that suits the audience and the situation.

Chapter 8: Presentation or Conversation? The Style of Delivery

Review Exercises

- **Be Prepared**—do advance work ahead of any speech, talk, or presentation
- **Down Cold**—ensure memorization of opening remarks to navigate adrenalin rush
- **Style Selection**—research in advance to meet audience expectations
- **Observation-Impact-Suggestion**—technique for effective critique
- **Practice Rehearsal for Effective Q&A with Active Listening**—get in shape
- **Keep the Conversation Going**—manage aggressive questions

Exercise Name	Frequency Goal / Actual	Observations	Next Steps
Keep the Conversation Going	Next upcoming presentation	Made Q&A much less stressful	Bring those questions to team meetings
	/		
	/		
	/		
	/		
	/		

Exercise Name	Frequency Goal / Actual	Observations	Next Steps
	/		
	/		
	/		
	/		
	/		
	/		

What Is Your *What?*
Connecting with Yourself

"Normal is getting dressed in clothes that you buy for work and driving through traffic in a car that you are still paying for—in order to get to the job you need to pay for the clothes and the car, and the house you leave vacant all day so you can afford to live in it."

—ELLEN GOODMAN

John, after working as an external consultant for a corporation, was then hired by that corporation to "come inside." He quickly discovered that the expertise he'd brought to the company as an external player, and for which he thought he'd been hired, was in fact the last thing the corporation now wanted from him. There was a grace period, during which as a new hire he was expected to get up to speed on a wide range of subjects. As he did so, however, he uncovered a multitude of issues that as a consultant he would have addressed. But now as an internal employee, he had no say over the critical issues he discovered. Needless to say, he was unhappy.

"What have I done?" he asked me again and again. With two kids under the age of four, he had the financial urgency of being the breadwinner. "I've only been inside a year. I can't just hop out now. It'll look bad on my résumé." He continued, "If I speak up about what I see, it'll go on my performance review and be on my permanent record. I'm stuck. I'm miserable."

He was boxed in by the double whammy of financial responsibility and the fear of speaking up, and his body was beginning to manifest the symptoms of chronic stress. His brow was tight and carried an always-worried expression; his posture was crumpled; his voice had a flattened, passionless tone. He was all of 31.

When trapped by unforeseen circumstances, the impact on communication, thinking, and productivity can be legion. John was stuck on every level. His verbal communication was timid and indecisive; his physical body was tense and his thinking muddled. As I listened to him and observed the signals he was sending, I thought about the book *The Code of the Executive* and its focus on mortality. I said to John that the position in which he found himself was one that demanded his greatest courage. He was not happy to hear this. Everyone is a leader, whether of his or her own life, small business, team, family, or even blog! And like it or not, life is short. Furthermore, observing how stress, fear, and negative emotions were impacting his life, it was essential that he find ways to realign his current reality with his intentions and aspirations.

I suggested that John key-message himself, that he list and then prioritize all the aspects that make him him. His *whats* could be literal (father, son, husband, manager) and behavioral (collaborator, idea generator, extrovert). I suggested the list be made over several weeks to allow his conscious and subconscious to contribute. Our priorities change almost daily, as one day being a manager feels most important, while the next, being a parent staying home to care for a sick child takes priority. Nonetheless, in the process of defining oneself in terms of all the roles played and how one accomplishes what one does (delegates, listens, instructs, orders, researches, makes dinner), a picture begins to emerge. What takes precedence? What comes last on the list? Where is the most time spent? The "Why" column usually articulates one's values, intentions, and purpose, and though that column is last on the form, it is usually what informs our deepest aspirations.

By clearly identifying our *whats*—the given roles that we play and core values that we hold dear—followed by the ways that we do what we do in order to achieve our hoped-for goals, it becomes easier to design and set direction for current situations and begin to conceptualize our next steps. It is also an excellent way to identify where our values and style either match or conflict with our given circumstances. As John so clearly manifested, a long-term mismatch can have significant impact on one's mind, body, and spirit.

TRY THIS: KEY-MESSAGE YOU

Using the key message template in the previous chapter, make multiple copies and scatter them around your office and home. Over several days or weeks, randomly jot down, as they occur to you, all the roles that you play and qualities that define your personality and style, followed by how you do what you do and your *why*, or the values that drive all your behaviors. By having multiple lists scattered randomly, you can write things down as you think of or observe them. After a couple of weeks, bring all the lists together and create one master key message template. Title it! (Hard but fascinating.) State your purpose for creating it and prioritize every listed item in order of importance. Put that master list away for a week or so and then take it out and review, edit or reprioritize it accordingly.

TRY THIS: WHAT DOES THE BODY THINK?

When you review the key message of you, notice what you feel in your body as you consider what you have written. Does a certain *how* or *what* make you feel excited in your belly, happy in your heart? Pay attention to the way your body reacts to your aspirations.

When trapped by circumstances that feel beyond our control, our tendency is to hunker down, avoid conflict, fly beneath the radar, and wait it out. Those choices or behaviors can be effective for a time. All of us at certain times must choose how to get through challenging circumstances, how to bite the bullet, as the expression goes. That's life! Our goals and values cannot always be in perfect alignment with our circumstances. Everything is situational. The cost varies depending on the circumstance, but in general, long-term submission to circumstances that are in deep conflict with our values may result in physical symptoms, emotional distress, and personal dissatisfaction.

Key-messaging oneself along with the practices of tuned-in body awareness as described in Part I may reveal levels of stress and unhappiness or great joy and satisfaction. Either way, if, as the captain of your personal ship, you feel lost at sea or buffeted by currents beyond your control, attempting to plot a strategy for addressing such is not only helpful; it can provide renewed passion and excitement. Often just the exercise itself helps to make a difficult situation more manageable because it allows you to imagine and implement different strategies and responses. Change rarely happens overnight. Shifts of direction, role, even style require patience, new thinking, new behaviors, help seeking, networking, and a whole host of tactics. Just by actively thinking about how to set a new course for the ship of *SS YOU*, you may discover that feeling trapped begins to dissipate and new tactics and strategies for engagement come to mind.

TRY THIS: WHAT IF I . . . ?

Make a list, similar to the one below, and sketch out any answers that pop into your mind. If there is a mismatch at work, this exercise will help you look at your current circumstances and provide options for responses.

"What if I . . .

speak up?"
say no?"
push back?"
agree?"
just wait?"
find an ally?"

start a campaign?"

quit my job?"

create a new network?"

Our choices are often far beyond what we imagine them to be, and with the daily consciousness that time is short, current circumstances might not seem so limiting.

TRY THIS: WHAT IF I . . . ?, CONTINUED

Building on the skills of body awareness, note what you feel in your body when you make your list of "what-ifs." Do you get tense? If so, where in your body do you feel the tension? Do you feel excited? If so, where? Scared? Where? The feelings may be very subtle, almost indecipherable. That's OK. The practice of noticing them will improve over time.

Increasingly our economy is made up of small businesses. Below are statistics from SBA.gov from the past few years:

The 23 million small businesses in America account for 54% of all U.S. sales. Small businesses provide 55% of all jobs and 66% of all net new jobs since the 1970s.

- The 600,000 plus franchised small businesses in the U.S. account for 40% of all retail sales and provide jobs for some 8 million people.
- The small business sector in America occupies 30–50% of all commercial space, an estimated 20–34 billion square feet.

Furthermore, the small business sector is growing rapidly. While corporate America has been "downsizing," the rate of small business "start-ups" has grown, and the rate for small business failures has declined.

- The number of small businesses in the United States has increased 49% since 1982.
- Since 1990, as big business eliminated 4 million jobs, small businesses added 8 million new jobs.

These are fascinating and inspiring statistics. The range of opportunities outside the corporate sphere is increasing. This is not to say that corporations are not viable workplaces; it's to demonstrate that there's a much wider work landscape than is immediately obvious. How the choice is made whether to steer toward a corporate role or a small or midsized business can often be the result of chance. A job is needed; an opening is pursued. Key-messaging yourself well in advance of the pursuit of a new job or, if you are employed, taking on that new project will more likely increase alignment with your core aspirations. Key-messaging yourself is also a good way of weeding out pursuits or work projects for which you're ill-suited. By defining what attracts and interests you and updating it as needed, you'll tune in to the opportunities that better resonate with your aspirations. Aspirations that align with your current situation are signaled by the body, just as those that don't align are communicated as well.

TRY THIS: GO FOR A WALK

You've titled your key message, prioritized your *whats*, identified how and why you do those *whats*. Now, go outside for a walk. Why? Walking is a great way to have the mind and body work in concert, to consider things from both cognitive and physical aspects. While walking, just let the mind wander. You've key-messaged yourself, you've created a conscious aspirational template. Trust that by allowing the body to move in space and time with that aspirational goal now clearly defined things will in time become clearer. Just going for a walk is one of the best things you can do for yourself. I keep hearing that sitting is the new smoking. My response? Walking is the newest (and oldest) cure.

In the theater there are good actors, gifted geniuses, so-so talents, mediocre wannabes. It is similar in every field. Despite all levels of skill and talent, from my perspective, actors come in two basic categories. There are those who act because they crave attention, need desperately to be loved, and seek constant reinforcement for their delicate egos. Then there are those who see themselves in a service profession. In other words, there are those who act to get and those who act to give. Everyone is a mixture of each, but the percentages can be significant. Those who act to give offer their skill, intelligence, passion, and emotion to *serve* the play and thereby give the *audience* an experience. They do not perform for their own self-aggrandizement, but to offer themselves to something greater than themselves. This doesn't mean they are egoless or have no opinions. Not at all! It means that the driving force behind their work is service.

Service can be performed at the highest levels of industry or the lowest levels of employment. With the exception of the 1 percent, almost everyone needs a paycheck. That's a given. How one conceptualizes contribution and reward can profoundly impact one's level of satisfaction and one's style of communication. Does the hospital orderly who mops the floors feel like a contributor or a wage slave? He or she may not have the skill to cure patients, but a few kind words said at the beside of an ill person can work miracles for both! Why is this important? From my perspective, it goes back to how we connect with ourselves and with others—how our work and actions resonate beyond their immediate impact, creating ripples of generative energy. Imagine how the orderly who sees his or her job as service will communicate to a patient.

What is service? It is putting oneself in the role of giving, irrespective of what comes back. It is giving for the sake of itself. It can happen anywhere, anytime, at work, at home, on the street. It is a mindset that once embraced can completely change one's point of view from victim to victor. Why victor? Because one cannot lose when in service. The clients or audiences may reject what is offered; that is their choice. But the offering itself is its own reward. When resonance, meaning, and service are all aligned, it shows. Managers, colleagues, and clients can feel that energy, and they connect with it and you.

Bodies can intuit this energy in the same way they instinctively intuit danger. In terms of presenting, if the talk is a gift versus a get, the experience for both speaker and audience will be altered radically.

Everyone is a client. I'm constantly amazed by those who are incredibly polite, deferential, and kind to external clients—and then beat the crap out of their own employees. It's akin to the star, so noble and gracious while receiving the standing ovation, but a horror to everyone backstage. Divas are tolerated, but only for so long. Bad behavior ultimately catches up with them, and their opportunities decrease. There are always rare exceptions for those who are so extraordinarily gifted that their less-than-stellar behavior will be tolerated. Most of us do not dwell in that heady atmosphere. Presence is for *always* and in *all* conditions. Of course, there will always be highly stressful, extenuating circumstances when we cannot be on our best behavior. We are humans and we mess up. But to be one way with the presumed "important" person and radically different with the less or "unimportant" one reveals the ultimate truth of one's values. We create hierarchies, and we decide who is important and deserves our respect. Hierarchical thinking and behavior is essential for many systems. There can only be one captain of a ship. Nonetheless that captain who treats visiting dignitaries like they are minigods and the engine crew like they are bugs suffers from a profound illusion. We are all on this ship together, each playing a vital part. Everyone we encounter deserves our kindness and respect.

When work is conceived as service and everyone is a client, the fetishism of who is greater or lesser dissolves, and one's sense of purpose is radically transformed. Each encounter can be an opportunity to discover something new, to listen with greater attention, be more present. It is hard after years and years of accumulating knowledge, education, wealth, and prestige to sacrifice ownership and admit that all these aspects have been borrowed by your brain to be offered to the world. But indeed, knowing and living this point of view removes vast amounts of suffering for oneself and those with whom one lives and works. Less ego, more connection, happier bodies.

> ## TRY THIS: THREE-ACT PLAY
>
> Think of three actions that you can take at work that will help a completely random person, not your boss! Then go to work and *do* them! How does that act impact the way you connect and communicate?

RESPECTING OR LIKING

The simple truth is that there are people we do not like. There are people we actively dislike. There are people we loathe. There are people who, for whatever reason, do not like us. Liking and disliking are human and cannot be avoided. For everyone, these highly charged feelings impact the body.

Many clients worry that if they push back, create clear boundaries, don't comply with every demand, they won't be liked. The boss won't like them; their colleagues won't like them. They spend vast amounts of time worrying about the consequences of speaking up or delivering difficult news. This seems to me to be an outgrowth of a strange contradiction that we all must learn to accept while growing up. When we were three or four and we hogged a toy, the parent or teacher said, "It's Sally's turn to have the toy now. You've had it a long time." We clutched the toy and refused to let it go. "Come on now, be nice. It's not fair that you've had the toy all this time and Sally hasn't. We have to be fair." Niceness and fairness were concepts that were drilled into our heads repeatedly as grown-up after grown-up insisted upon our compliance. Then we entered high school, and suddenly we encountered the not-so-nice kid at the next desk who pulled all As and never cracked a book, or the one who got all the hot dates and yet treated girls like used furniture. "Life isn't fair" became the new mantra that parents and teachers drilled over and over again, attempting to prepare us for the fact that, indeed, it isn't. "But what about being nice, being liked?" shouts the inner four-year-old who spent years tamping down the greedy infantile self in order to be nice and fair. This contradiction seems to plague us for the rest of our days. Then we have children, and we repeat the contradiction all over again for them!

Of course we must socialize and civilize our children, so that we can all live and, the hope is, thrive within our given societies. Every culture does and has done this throughout history. Different concepts regarding life are laid down at different ages depending on the maturity of the child. But each of those concepts and contradictions functions *within* us continually. The unconscious doesn't know time. The subconscious doesn't know that what was learned at 4 is any less or more true than what was learned at 24. All have equal weight and veracity in it. Despite our *neo*cortex (*neo* as in "new") using reason, logic, and life experience to assess the current reality, the subconscious maintains its power and pull. The inner fight between being taught so young to be nice and fair, only to discover that life has no such concept, results in a constant tug-of-war between the rational and the irrational, the imaginary and the real. And fairness is merely one single concept with which we all struggle! The compromise many make is to focus excessively on being liked.

"If I do that, so-and-so won't like me."

"And?" I ask.

"They'll make things more difficult for me down the line."

"And?"

"Then, I'll have to work around that."

"And?"

"I might be able to work around that. I'm not sure, though."

Very often we get stuck at "he or she won't like me," and at that point, fearing conflict—it is the very rare person who actually likes conflict—we impinge on our ideas or actions. We stop ourselves out of fear of not being liked. "Finish the fantasy" is my constant refrain. We often stop at the point of conflict and leave it at that. Instead, practice "What if?"

TRY THIS: FINISH THE FANTASY

Think of a recent work conflict with someone with whom you do not get along or whom you actively dislike. Write down the complete fantasy of what might happen if you performed the task about which you were anxious. No matter what the consequence or conflict, keep writing a response to whatever imagined obstacle comes your way. Don't stop. Take it as far into left field as you like—it's *your* fantasy!

TRY THIS: FINISH THE FANTASY, CONTINUED

Tune into the somatic body response to what you have created above. Do you feel energized, anxious, excited, happy? Where in your body do you feel those reactions?

The goal of the above is to permit your imagination to take you out of the limiting frame of being liked to explore other possible consequences. The outcome may be totally unrealistic or outrageous, or it may be quite pragmatic. The eventual outcome is less important than the action of completing the fantasy. It is a conversation with yourself to explore where you place limits on your own sense of agency out of the fear of not being liked, and the impact on your body from doing so.

More critical than being liked is being respected. People respect those who live by their values, do the best they can, and treat others with respect. Those who respect themselves are often indifferent to being liked. Everyone would prefer to be liked; it simply feels better. Most of us are pleasers; it's only human. (And in evolutionary terms, probably ensured our survival.) But those who seek respect are willing to lose the popularity contest. They are willing to suffer the consequences of living their truth. That's not to say that they are unkind. They can be very kind, respectful, even deferential, but they are indifferent to being liked and thus able to take greater risks and communicate with courage.

TRY THIS: WHICH DOMINATES, BEING LIKED OR RESPECTED?

Make a list of those you know at work who fall into one of the categories above. Who is worried about being liked more than respected? Who is indifferent to being liked? Who has a good balance of each? When you return to the office, take some time to observe those on your lists and make note of how they move, walk, talk, gesture, and express themselves. What do you observe? Can you draw any parallels to your own body as an instrument with regard to being liked or respected?

BUILDING RELATIONSHIPS

When work is performing service, solving problems, and helping others, people notice! If indeed the notion of hierarchy is suspended and everyone is treated with kindness and respect, extraordinary things begin to occur. Those who create a collaborative atmosphere of "We're all in this together" attract others who feel similarly. (While those who thrive on power, hierarchy, and external approbation also attract their kind. Like finds like. Interestingly, I've found that people who grow up in very strict, rigid families tend to wind up working for very strict, rigid companies. It's what they are used to. It mirrors what they've known and feels familiar. *Family* is the root of *familiar*.)

Whatever the culture of your organization may be, all enterprises depend on relationships. We need each other to get things accomplished. We are also constantly building up a database of information about each other that is comprised of all encounters, both random and purposeful. When asked who on a team is the whiner, the know-it-all, or the yes-man, there is hardly a moment of hesitation about who would be cast for each role. Such meta-characteristics are intuited by all and build up layer by layer from repeated encounters and behaviors. Due to the amplification effect, they are then gossiped about, and the reputation spreads further. We read each other constantly, pretty much instantly, and irrefutably. Once that initial data has been stored, it is almost impossible to scrap it from the hard drive that is your primal brain. (We are loath to disagree with our own first impressions.) Over time bad behavior can be forgiven, especially if the person apologizes and makes good on ways to remediate. Relationships are not static. Neither are we. We are dynamic and can alter in profound ways. Nonetheless, first impressions are built upon, not erased. So if you are aware of any missteps that may have hindered how people feel about you and might impact work flow, take steps to remedy them. Reach out; apologize; ask for feedback; communicate. Building a network, a web of people who know your values, respect your work, and see you as a contributor, is an essential part of doing business.

TRY THIS: THE WEB OF YOU

Make a chart of the people you know with whom you work, putting yourself in the center and creating concentric circles out from that center in order of depth of relationship. Those placed closest to you might be your immediate boss, colleagues, reports; then move outward to two steps removed, then three, etc. (You can make one for your personal life as well.) As an exercise, this can be a revelation! It can show you the deep web of life and connection of which you are a part, the places where repair is needed, the relationships that have faded or deepened. Why do this? Because relationships are our glue. They place us in or out of dynamic circulation. They keep us stuck or open up amazing possibilities. But we need to see where we sit in this dynamic and understand how we enable or disable our potential.

TRY THIS: WEB SIX DEGREES OF SEPARATION

Take a person from your network of coworkers, friends, or family. Put this person in the center of the circle and, to the best of your knowledge and ability, do the same exercise from his or her perspective. Whom does this person put first, second, third in his or her expanding concentric circles? Whom does he or she need in order to thrive and feel connected? Why do this? It may help you to understand the choices that this person has made that have enabled or hobbled his or her potential.

We live in an intricate web of relationships that expands widely from our nexus into the world. How we value, respect, build, and treasure those relationships will greatly enhance our ability to communicate, connect—and serve.

Chapter 9: What Is Your *What?* Connecting with Yourself

Review Exercises

- **Key-Message You**—self, values, goal alignment
- **What Does the Body Think?**—how the body reflects our aspirations
- **What If I . . . ?**—capacity for risk
- **What If I . . . ?, Continued**—imagination
- **Go for a Walk** —self-reflection
- **Three-Act Play**—service
- **Finish the Fantasy**—courage
- **Finish the Fantasy, Continued**—risk, courage, imagination
- **Which Dominates, Being Liked or Respected?**—self-awareness
- **The Web of You**—relationship awareness
- **Web Six Degrees of Separation**—understanding the impact of relationships

Exercise Name	Frequency Goal / Actual	Observations	Next Steps
Finish the Fantasy	When worried about a work conflict	I imagined things that made me feel much braver and less anxious	See if there is a way I can actually implement some of my courageous ideas
	/		
	/		
	/		
	/		

Exercise Name	Frequency Goal / Actual	Observations	Next Steps
	/		
	/		
	/		
	/		
	/		
	/		

Connecting
in a Virtual World

"For a list of all the ways technology has failed to improve the quality of life, please press three."

—ALICE KAHN

Increasingly, at large national and global companies, meetings happen virtually. A group of people gather in a video-enabled meeting room to discuss projects and challenges, give updates, and work together. The technology is constantly evolving, and new approaches to this phenomenon appear daily. One attempt to improve engagement is a technology that creates an avatar for each participant, making virtual encounters more gamelike. No doubt, more inventions will emerge and grow in popularity. Telephone conferences, where participants can only be heard but not seen, are increasingly common. The constant complaint I hear from my clients is that these technologies, while created to enable people to work together, are themselves obstacles to effectively connecting. One frequent syndrome: people, when asked to attend long, meandering teleconferences, push the mute button and, until called upon, ignore what's going on, thereby missing the whole point of being on the phone.

The challenge, as I and many others see it, is that we evolved over hundreds of thousands of years to read each other's microsignals in real time, moment by changing moment. A briefly raised eyebrow, the flash of a smile, a quick frown, a head nod, these are all very important signals. They can either move a discussion forward or cause it to pause. Imagine someone nodding to indicate "I understand" verses "I agree." It's the same gesture, with totally different meanings, each communicated via highly nuanced motions in mere fractions of a second. Add to this the impact on our mirror neurons, as discussed previously, when we are not together in space and time. As a result, its almost impossible to assess how much is missed by disabling our neural WiFi. All this is to say, navigating virtual meetings is a serious challenge. (I have no doubt that in some lab, engineers and scientists are working to invent a system the will allow for micro-autonomic responses to be recorded and exchanged virtually!)

With increased globalization and tight travel budgets, the use of technologies that create the illusion of being together will only increase. As of now, virtual meeting rooms simply cannot provide the cohesion and visual clarity that happens when people gather together. What to do?

First, for those meetings that simply cannot happen any other way, whoever calls the meeting needs to set crystal-clear expectations and boundaries ahead of time. The topics to be covered should be put in an agenda and time frames for each topic clearly delineated. At the launch of a virtual or phone meeting, a structure should be clearly articulated. For example, the meeting leader might open with the following remarks: "Welcome, everyone. Thanks for joining. We'll be on this call for 25 minutes. The first 5 minutes will be an update by John Smith. That will be followed by 5 minutes for questions. Then we will have 10 minutes to discuss and answer any questions you may have about the deck that was sent out to all of you last week from Sue Jones. Please have your questions ready, and queue up on the left of your screen. Following Sue, we will have an open-ended 5-minute discussion on the proposal I sent out to all of you. I want to know what the risks and benefits are from your perspective. Please keep your comments brief and targeted. If you have other thoughts about the proposal outside the framework for today, feel free to send those to all of us, and we will put them on the agenda for our next meeting. Thank you, and now, John, over to you."

By clearly articulating the goals and time frames, the participants' brains are primed and focused. People will know why they are there and what is expected of them. Once such a structure is in place, it must be adhered to. If 5 minutes is allotted to John Smith and that part of the conversation goes on for 10, people will know it, feel it, and resent it. Stick to the structure, and in time, it will train everyone to step into it with greater ease.

Reasons for meetings vary. Some are casual or just for updates and brainstorming, but even those can be structured in a way that helps mitigate the challenges of not being all together in space and time.

TRY THIS: VIRTUAL OR REAL: KEY-MESSAGE A MEETING

What is the purpose of the meeting? What is the most critical *what* to discuss? How much time will be allotted to it? Will there be Q&A? If so, how much time will be provided for that? Who will speak, when, and on what subject? How much time for each? Will there be free-form discussion or not? Who will facilitate that discussion? Create an agenda but, beyond that, design the format and structure, and e-mail both ahead of time to all participants. After the meeting, find out what worked and where the structure could have been improved. Seek the opinions of those on the call. This may feel constrained. Ironically, structure creates freedom; when there are no clear boundaries and everything is up for grabs, that's when people get impatient, when they feel that their time is being wasted, or when one person feels entitled to hog the meeting.

For virtual meetings it's critical to be conscious of your movements and facial expressions. Depending on the technology, transmission of speech and gestures can sometimes be delayed. Be aware of where the camera and microphones are so that you don't turn your face away from the very thing that is transmitting your voice. Lean toward the microphone to make sure what you say is captured, and be aware that off-the-record comments can be heard as well. Different systems show people in different configurations: some capture each person in his or her own little box; others capture an entire conference table. No matter how the information is delivered, once you are live, you are indeed "on" and often on permanent record.

In a face-to-face meeting, you know instantly when someone is looking at you. That's not so obvious in a virtual meeting. Where you put your focus needs to be practiced, since eyes looking at a screen and not a person can feel oddly disembodied. And for such things as meetings over a computer, not a video system, there is the added challenge that the camera eye on a computer is usually above the screen. Do you look at the camera, which will appear to the recipients as though you are looking at them? Or do you look at the screen, so you can see who the other participants are and what their faces and bodies are showing? It's good to develop a practice of switching back and forth so that you will appear to be making occasional eye contact with your viewers. Learning how to be "present" in a virtual meeting demands increased levels of focus.

When participating in lengthy telephone conferences, additional things need to be kept top of mind. When a call drags on and on, people tend to become disengaged, and vocal energy flags. Voices become monotone, fillers creep in, and listeners tune out. When on a teleconference, make sure that when you do speak, your voice has energy, vitality, melody, and very distinct pitch variation. Your voice is all that you will have to deliver your content. Make sure your vocal delivery is aligned with your purpose. Know ahead of time what your purpose is. Is it to convince, influence, educate, question, or debate? Tone and energy are aligned with intention, so make sure yours is clear.

I've been asked many times, "How do I know when to speak?" There are often two- to three-second delays when people speak, and it is hard to know if they are thinking or finished talking. People tell me they don't want to interrupt, but then wind up doing so due to the time delay.

If the technology causes delays, it is good at the start of the meeting to suggest ways to work with that challenge. Acknowledge that due to transmission time it may appear that someone is finished when in fact he or she is not. Suggest that people use either a hand gesture or head nod to indicate they are finished speaking if video is being used. If there is only voice transmission, conclude with a brief phrase, such as, "That's all" or "I'm finished." Another technique is to establish the practice that everyone internally count to two seconds after someone has spoken to prevent overtalk or interruption. These will feel awkward at first but will become routine. I've gotten multiple reports from my clients who've employed these techniques that they work very well.

SMILE! YOU'RE ON CAMERA

We are living in a world where increasingly we are visible wherever we go. Ubiquitous phone cameras, not to mention surveillance technologies, can and do capture off-the-cuff sound and video clips and project private moments onto the World Wide Web. This is not to say we must succumb to an "on-all-the-time" persona. It is to say that we must at all times be genuinely who we are and be acutely aware that our behavior matters. These days almost all business conferences are videotaped, not just the keynote speakers but the leadership team, sales force, people on panel discussions—you name it. Google a professional and chances are you'll find images and/or video of him or her online. Even informal meetings, because of videoconferencing, are often permanently on record as well. Awareness of this cultural shift is as crucial as is practicing.

Actors rehearse; athletes run drills; teachers write lesson plans; surgeons do mental run-throughs. What do you do on a regular basis to keep your messaging clear, concise, and credible? Do you practice? Do you imagine who your audience members will be and what they'll need to know?

TRY THIS: SPEAK THE SPEECH FOR VIRTUAL COMMUNICATION

Virtual meetings create additional layers of distance that are best overcome by *clarity*. As previously discussed, clarity is almost impossible to achieve without practice. Practice out loud an upcoming virtual deliverable. These meetings are often around a conference table. If possible, arrive at the space ahead of time to see where the camera is. Make sure you place your notes, computer, or any other materials in a position that will not require you to turn your face away from the camera or microphone when referencing them. Imagine a question and answer it. Practice embedding places for questions or two-second holds for transmission delay. Practice a slower pace and crisp enunciation as ways to manage the time delay.

Most of our conversations and interactions cannot be rehearsed because they happen in the now. Managing the ever-shifting realities of that now, being able to form and articulate rapid responses without any prior thought, is a key indicator of how you think and who you are. Listening, humor, kindness, creativity, originality, service, intention, point of view, word choice, focusing out—all these aspects of your style—are made manifest in your moment-to-moment behaviors and responses. All these actions are expressed through your body. But video lives beyond the moment. And while it cannot capture all aspects of subtext and atmosphere, it is best not to be caught off-guard. Your presence, how you manage the moment, now lives on virtually. Awareness that everything done electronically has the potential to live on indefinitely must always be top of mind.

TRY THIS: WRITE; DON'T SEND

There is simply no substitute for a good night's sleep to help calm down the impulse to "react." The accusatory e-mail arrives, and now fully engaged, you jump to respond, usually defensively or by blaming someone else. Go ahead: Write that e-mail! (Make sure you leave the address bar blank.) Type that text. Get it out of your system. Then, *don't* send it. Put it in Drafts and take a break. As technology demands faster and faster turnaround times, it pushes us to react without thought. Print out the e-mail and imagine yourself receiving it. Chances are, you'll wind up tossing it.

When writing e-mails, make sure your language is clear. Something as simple as defining an acronym, which seems unnecessary and time consuming, can be vitally important. A client of mine was once engaged in a *two-week* e-mail exchange—read "battle"—because her understanding of a widely used company acronym had a completely different meaning to her recipient who worked at the same company but in a different business unit. Two weeks of increasingly hostile back-and-forth e-mails could have been averted if she'd been clear from the very start.

Much has been written about tone in e-mails and how such things as sarcasm and irony can be wildly misinterpreted. Given the fact that many business professionals can receive hundreds of e-mails a day, do everything possible to make yours clear, short, and polite while appreciating that different cultures have different expectations. In the United States we are expected to get right to the point, but in many other cultures that is considered rude. In Europe an e-mail that doesn't open with a warm salutation, or with a question about how the recipient is doing, may be off-putting. Some cultures feel that opening with just the word *I*, as in "I wonder if you agree with the e-mail that went out earlier?," is unacceptable. Similar to becoming familiar with a culture before meeting a new colleague from another country, it is a good practice to learn the appropriate e-mail etiquette for an unfamiliar business recipient.

There is, and will continue to be for the foreseeable future, an ongoing challenge between those who grew up before the web and digital natives. One might imagine this would be resolved as those "elders" leave the workforce, but judging by how quickly technology changes, I think this will be an ongoing situation. Teachers will always be around 20 to 25 years older than their students. That's a generation. No matter what those teachers grew up with, you can be certain that the children they will be teaching will have grown up with something entirely different. This will not be exclusive to education, but to work in general. The technological revolution is indeed a revolution. It never stops revolving, evolving, and completely changing our experience of time. Now dial-up seems painfully slow. (For those who don't even know what dial-up is, Google it!) Expectations are created by prior experiences, and given that there will always be at minimum two decades between those established in the workplace and the new generation entering it, this will be a constant challenge.

Life, however, moves at its own pace. Bodies do, too. We evolved to comprehend the world at the pace that life moves. Visual information—light, color, motion—enters through the cornea, and then the cells in the retina convert that information into electrical impulses that are sent, via the optic nerve, to the brain, where an image of that visual input is produced. Repeated information traveling that route actually creates the formation of the nerve. Infant eyesight evolved over hundreds of thousands of years to track a person as he or she moved across space *in human time, not video game time.*

Human *behaviors* have adjusted and changed as technology has increased our travel, information, and communication systems, but human *beings* still run on biological time. We still require food, sleep, movement, rest. We live in bodies that, no matter how they've adjusted to cars that drive 80 miles per hour or tweets that can instantaneously be read by thousands around the world, still run on human time.

I am a body person. I believe that the human body is our source of knowledge, joy, connection, experience, thought, memory, imagination, fear, love, and spirit. It houses us and gives us existence. Smell, touch, taste, sight, and sound—the five senses—are our connection to this life, the lives around us, and the world we inhabit. The cognitive scientist Guy Claxton puts it beautifully, and I will quote him here:

> Through the body I am deeply ecological, profoundly and ceaselessly in conversation with the physical and the social milieu in which I am embedded (and from which I am continually emerging). Like the wave, I am made up—concocted—by the world around me. Like a mobile phone, I may look like a lump of stuff, but I am actually aquiver with information—whether I am currently checking myself for messages or not. So says the science of embodiment. (From the RSA presentation "On Being Touched and Moved," November 26, 2013, www.thersa.org/discover/videos/event-videos/2013/11/on-being-touched-and-moved/.)

Don't get me wrong; I enjoy technology. I love that the world's libraries are now at my fingertips, that I can Skype with a friend on the other side of the planet, and that I can go on YouTube to discover how to fix just about anything! But I also know that it is my body in real time—listening, engaging, *be-ing*, and connecting with others—that creates this life.

Your communication expertise and your presence are composed of the quality of time, attention, and focus you give to others, the quality of your ideas and suggestions, the quality of your listening. We are all the outcomes of decades, resting upon centuries, of observing, learning, thinking, breathing, experiencing. We compose our lives, adding layer upon layer of experience, memory, intuition, knowledge. The tapestry that evolves is profoundly complex.

However you choose to communicate via technology, remember that chances are it will be a permanent record that will never fully capture the complex layers of knowledge, experience, intuition, and relationships you have built over a lifetime. Virtual connection can and does add wonderful new layers of communication, relationships, and knowledge. Just remember to keep a balanced approach. Leave your computer; put down your phone; take a walk; talk to colleagues face-to-face; leave your desk to eat your lunch. These are such simple things to do, but hard to maintain.

When there is no choice but to connect through virtual meetings, pay greater attention to the signals sent as bodies and subtext will be harder to read, and vocal tone will be harder to distinguish. If the meeting consists of people from different cultures with different languages, make sure that you are clear on the points being made. Never assume a nod means yes, unless you get clarification. If a gesture is hard to interpret, don't assume. Ask.

Chapter 10: Connecting in a Virtual World

Review Exercises

- **Virtual or Real: Key-Message a Meeting**—prime to keep participant focus and attention when not together physically
- **Speak the Speech for Virtual Communication**—prep for delivery, speech, panel discussion that may be recorded
- **Write; Don't Send**—discharge reaction, give yourself time to think

Exercise Name	Frequency Goal / Actual	Observations	Next Steps
Write Don't Send	Whenever I'm too reactive	Cooling off really helped!	Keep doing it!
	/		
	/		
	/		
	/		
	/		

EPILOGUE
Putting It All Together

A fter years of classes in voice, movement, scene study, character work, and text analysis, actors enter the theater world trained and ready to work. They audition as much as possible, always in hope of landing a role, but also with the full knowledge that statistically their chances are slim at best. Still, they try out again and again. They are almost never told why they don't get a role. Often it can be due to something as uncontrollable as an actress being three inches taller than the previously cast male lead. When actors are hired, they enter a company usually of strangers, all of whom may have very different techniques and approaches to rehearsal and acting itself. Some actors memorize all their lines before they step into the rehearsal room; others don't know their lines until the first public preview.

What is the job of the director? A good director casts well and then creates a safe space where failure, experimentation, risk taking, and varied approaches are encouraged, where each actor feels heard, attended to, protected, supported, and encouraged. Actors are hired because of their gifts, smarts, and instincts, and to discover what their unique talents will bring to the interpretation of a character. A director may lead an actor into totally unexpected choices, and the actor may do the same with the director. An actor can reveal to a director an idea or interpretation that the director had never imagined. There is created in the company a pulling-and-pushing energy of ideas, experimentation, and risk. Eventually, the "family" is formed, the "team" is made, these disparate parts are made into a whole, and the show opens.

The theater is not unique in this. Company announcements, mergers, brand launches, commercial campaigns—all businesses have their versions of opening night, but few have such systematic rehearsal techniques and processes. Make no mistake; actors have egos, and with high-stakes careers on the line, there can be ugly backstage politics. Given the enormous obstacles to success—the extraordinary vulnerability of the process, untried players, the harshness of the press, fickle audience tastes, a new untested script—it is quite a miracle that any production becomes a hit. But a great team, if smartly pulled together, knows it is there to serve the play and serve the audience. Ultimately, that trumps all petty squabbles. How often does that happen? As rarely as it does in the "real" world. But it happens. And when it does, it feels like a miracle—and in a way it is.

Often, when I've departed a team training at a large corporation and gotten an earful on the internal squabbles and high-stakes politics, I've wondered how the participants succeeded so well. It is always amazing, given bruised egos, unresolved infantile tendencies, and everyone's varying needs for attention, that anything is accomplished at all. But, in general, the trains do run on time; lights turn on; food gets to market; drugs get made. The miracle, as I see it, is that despite all of our incredibly complex challenges, we do find ways to pull together. We do focus; we do listen; we have powerful minds, open hearts, and smart guts. We care. Given the tools now at our disposal, we may usher the planet's and our future into long-lasting health and abundance. Or not. At root is the degree to which each of us can achieve compassion, mindfulness, service, and a willingness to imagine and play. My hope is that some of the ideas and suggestions in this book will assist you along the path of connecting with yourself and with others.

Success is utterly personal. It needs to be investigated deeply, quietly, in the dark of the night. The process that enables each person to find his or her passion, to develop all the skills needed to share and devote that passion toward work, play, and service, is never finished. This book was not written to instruct, but to engender a deep, ongoing practice of conversation. It is fun to play with imagination, self-conception, and the body as an instrument of connection. There is no single magic bullet that will align all apects of mind, body, emotion, and spirit; it is a lifelong process. It is my hope that by playing with the exercises suggested throughout this book, by experimenting and even making up your own, you'll discover all kinds of things about yourself that you may have never known.

I've one final suggestion: take an acting or improvisation class! The skills learned there—how to listen, to trust your gut, to build a team, to collaborate, to use your imagination, to offer yourself to the role, to serve, to connect, and to play—can be applied to *any* profession. Further, if you have a child, or know of any youngster between nine and college age, enroll or suggest to your friends or relatives to enroll that youngster in an acting, improvisation, or even theater games class. Team sports are a fantastic way to engender loyalty, strength, confidence, collaboration, to name just a few of the skills fostered there. But an acting class enables all that in addition to a whole host of other emotional, social, and spiritual skills not found in sports. Why not offer both?

There's a game often played by children in preschool in which they pretend to be animals—elephants, lions, monkeys, and such. You may have even done this when you were very young. If you were four or five, you likely did it with complete and total abandon and no sense of embarrassment or shame. It was fun. You didn't want to stop. When the teacher said, "OK, kids, time to sit down," you felt different, wonderful. You'd made fantastic sounds and gestures and experienced yourself in a new way. But not totally, because back then, your body was used to moving in all kinds of wonderful, unexpected, and amazing ways. What happened? You grew up. What about now? Can you play?

TRY THIS: BE AN ELEPHANT

Why not? No one's looking. Bend forward; make a trunk with your arms; let them swing low and then wave up; make an elephant trumpet call. Lumber around. Go ahead. Give it a try.

No? OK, here's another: play air guitar. Put on some music, stand up, and let yourself go. Too much for you? Then just skip. Remember learning to skip, how exciting that was? It should have been exciting because skipping is a real marker of growth. Only after connections between the right and left hemispheres and across the corpus callosum are formed can we skip. You were about five. So go ahead. Try it again. Skip for a bit. Let yourself feel and enjoy the amazing instrument that you are.

If all of the above are still asking too much, that's OK, although I hope that one day you'll let yourself try at least one of them. But even so, now that you know the power of thought, merely imagining yourself doing any of the above just for a few moments might be enough to illuminate the enlightening power of play.

APPENDIX A
Exercises by Chapter
in Order of Appearance

Chapter 1: Use Your Head
- Happy/Sad Mouth
- Sweet Apricot: Jaw Relax
- Head Hinge
- Broken Bridge
- Wet Dog
- Head Hinge with Voice
- Reverse Turtle Neck
- Star Eyes
- Just an Inch!
- Habit Breaker
- Mirror Talk
- Elephant Ears
- Inner Ear
- Take a Thought for a Walk
- Word Move
- Out Loud
- Judge's Journal
- Judge's Journal Replies
- Standing O

Chapter 2: Have a Heart
- Embodied Aspiration
- Embodied Ick
- The List of You
- The List of Your Nemesis
- Open Heart
- Right Words
- Tune In

- Stressful or Soothing
- Wet Dog Talking
- Tone Talk
- Subtle Subtext
- Subtle Text
- Hear Yourself
- Lazy Lips Workout
- Filler Be Gone!
- Fan Arms
- The Butterfly
- Weighted Neck Stretch
- Belly Breath
- Corner Speak
- 10-Second Breath
- Abdomen Vibrate
- Chest Vibrate
- Torso Vibrate
- Breath with Arm Thrust
- Get the Peanut Butter Off
- Hand Rest
- Hand Dance
- Hand Watch
- Body Scan
- Bag of Sand

Chapter 3: Gut Smarts
- Soft Belly
- Belly Imagine
- Belly Feel
- Tuning in to the Tuned Out

Chapter 4: Standing Tall
- Beach Walk
- Office Walk
- Seated Pelvic Tilt
- Belly Dance
- Open Hips
- Take a Thought for a Dance

- Feeling Feet
- Centering
- Launch
- Long Step/Short Step
- Sitting Tall
- Walk Copy
- Ministry of Silly Walks

Chapter 5: Center of Unconscious Gravity

- Center Control Towers
- Happy Shoulders/Sad Hips
- Happy Shoulders/Sad Feet While Presenting
- Lions, Tigers, Bears, . . . and Puppies
- Your Inner Animal
- Take It All In
- Focus On
- Focus On While Presenting
- Safe-Place Sense Memory

Chapter 6: Presence

- The Flow: A Toe in the Stream
- The Flow: Body *Now*
- The Flow: Mind *Now*
- The Seed of Failure
- What Did Failure Grow?
- Failure's Offspring
- What If . . . ?
- Write Your Hero a Letter
- Be Your Hero

Chapter 7: Designing Messages to Increase Presence

- Purpose and Audience
- What's the Title?
- Detail the Key Messages
- Metaphor/Simile Practice

Chapter 8: Presentation or Conversation? The Style of Delivery

- Be Prepared

APPENDIX B
Exercise Applications and Purposes

Please note that you may see the same exercise listed in multiple categories of application, as many exercises have several purposes and outcomes. To enable you to locate the exercise easily, the chapter number has been added in parentheses.

Active Listening
- Elephant Ears (1)
- Keep the Conversation Going (8)

Arms
- The Butterfly (2)
- Hand Rest (2)

Belly
- Abdomen Vibrate (2)
- Belly Breath (2)
- Belly Feel (3)
- Belly Imagine (3)
- Broken Bridge (1)
- Sitting Tall (4)
- Torso Vibrate (2)

Body Awareness
- Be Your Hero (6)
- Beach Walk (4)
- Belly Breath (2)
- Belly Feel (3)
- Body Scan (2)

- Broken Bridge (1)
- Center Control Towers (5)
- Embodied Aspiration (2)
- Embodied Ick (2)
- Feeling Feet (4)
- Hand Dance (2)
- Hand Watch (2)
- Happy Shoulders/Sad Feet While Presenting (5)
- The Flow: A Toe in the Stream (6)
- The Flow: Body *Now* (6)
- Focus On (5)
- Go for a Walk (9)
- Happy/Sad Mouth (1)
- Happy Shoulders/Sad Hips (5)
- Head Hinge (1)
- Hear Yourself (2)
- Just an Inch! (1)
- Long Step/Short Step (4)
- Ministry of Silly Walks (4)
- Mirror Talk (1)
- Office Walk (4)

- Practice Rehearsal for Effective Q&A with Active Listening (8)
- Seated Pelvic Tilt (4)
- Sitting Tall (4)
- Star Eyes (1)
- Stressful or Soothing (2)
- Take a Thought for a Walk (1)
- Tuning in to the Tuned Out (3)
- Walk Copy (4)
- Wet Dog Talking (2)
- What Does the Body Think? (9)
- What if I . . . ?, Continued (9)

Breathing
- Abdomen Vibrate (2)
- Belly Breath (2)
- Body Scan (2)
- Breath with Arm Thrust (2)
- Broken Bridge (1)
- Chest Vibrate (2)
- 10-Second Breath (2)
- Torso Vibrate (2)

Centering
- Be Prepared (8)
- Be Your Hero (6)
- Belly Breath (2)
- Body Scan (2)
- Broken Bridge (1)
- Centering (4)
- Down Cold (8)
- Elephant Ears (1)
- Embodied Aspiration (2)
- Get the Peanut Butter Off (2)
- Go for a Walk (9)
- Hand Rest (2)
- Head Hinge (1)
- Launch (4)

- Open Heart (2)
- Reverse Turtle Neck (1)
- Safe-Place Sense Memory (5)
- Sitting Tall (4)
- Standing O (1)
- Take It All In (5)
- 10-Second Breath (2)
- Torso Vibrate (2)

Chest
- Chest Vibrate (2)
- Fan Arms (2)
- Open Heart (2)

Confidence
- Be Prepared (8)
- Be Your Hero (6)
- Belly Breath (2)
- Breath with Arm Thrust (2)
- Broken Bridge (1)
- Center Control Towers (5)
- Centering (4)
- Corner Speak (2)
- Down Cold (8)
- Embodied Aspiration (2)
- Failure's Offspring (6)
- Fan Arms (2)
- Finish the Fantasy (9)
- Finish the Fantasy, Continued (9)
- Get the Peanut Butter Off (2)
- Go for a Walk (9)
- Head Hinge (1)
- Judge's Journal (1)
- Key-Message You (9)
- Launch (4)
- The List of You (2)
- Observation-Impact-Suggestion (8)

- Practice Rehearsal for Effective Q&A with Active Listening (8)
- Safe-Place Sense Memory (5)
- The Seed of Failure (6)
- Sitting Tall (4)
- Speak the Speech for Virtual Communication (10)
- Standing O (1)
- Style Selection (8)
- Take a Thought for a Dance (4)
- 10-Second Breath (2)
- The Web of You (9)
- Web Six Degrees of Separation (9)
- What Did Failure Grow? (6)
- What If I . . . ? (9)
- Which Dominates, Being Liked or Respected? (9)
- Word Move (1)
- Write Your Hero a Letter (6)

Connecting
- Body Scan (2)
- The Flow: Mind *Now* (6)
- Happy/Sad Mouth (1)
- Keep the Conversation Going (8)
- Open Heart (2)
- Practice Rehearsal for Effective Q&A with Active Listening (8)
- Right Words (2)
- Style Selection (8)
- Three-Act Play (9)
- Tone Talk (2)
- The Web of You (9)
- Web Six Degrees of Separation (9)

Creativity
- Be Your Hero (6)
- Belly Feel (3)

- Belly Imagine (3)
- Finish the Fantasy (9)
- Key-Message You (9)
- The List of You (2)
- Metaphor/Simile Practice (7)
- Ministry of Silly Walks (4)
- Safe-Place Sense Memory (5)
- Walk Copy (4)
- What If . . . ? (6)
- What's the Title? (7)
- Write Your Hero a Letter (6)

Delivery Preexercises for Presentation/Communication
- Be Prepared (8)
- Be Your Hero (6)
- Belly Breath (2)
- Body Scan (2)
- Breath with Arm Thrust (2)
- Centering (4)
- Corner Speak (2)
- Down Cold (8)
- Embodied Aspiration (2)
- Launch (4)
- Lazy Lips Workout (2)
- Key Message (7)
- Observation-Impact-Suggestion (8)
- Take a Thought for a Dance (4)
- Torso Vibrate (2)
- Virtual or Real: Key-Message a Meeting (10)

Design
- Key Message (7)
- Metaphor/Simile Practice (7)
- Practice Rehearsal for Effective Q&A with Active Listening (8)
- Purpose and Audience (7)

- Style Selection (8)
- Virtual or Real: Key-Message a Meeting (10)
- What's the Title? (7)

Embodiment

- Be Your Hero (6)
- Beach Walk (4)
- Belly Feel (3)
- Belly Imagine (3)
- Broken Bridge (1)
- Embodied Aspiration (2)
- Go for a Walk (9)
- Habit Breaker (1)
- Just an Inch! (1)
- Office Walk (4)
- Open Heart (2)
- Take a Thought for a Walk (1)
- Walk Copy (4)
- Which Dominates, Being Liked or Respected? (9)

Emotion-Body Feedback Loop

- Beach Walk (4)
- Broken Bridge (1)
- Center Control Towers (5)
- Embodied Aspiration (2)
- Embodied Ick (2)
- Fan Arms (2)
- Feeling Feet (4)
- Go for a Walk (9)
- Habit Breaker (1)
- Happy/Sad Mouth (1)
- Happy Shoulders/Sad Hips (5)
- Head Hinge (1)
- Long Step/Short Step (4)
- Ministry of Silly Walks (4)
- Office Walk (4)

- Sitting Tall (4)
- Soft Belly (3)
- Standing O (1)
- Star Eyes (1)
- Stressful or Soothing (2)
- Take a Thought for a Dance (4)
- Take a Thought for a Walk (1)
- Walk Copy (4)
- What if I . . . ?, Continued (9)

Executive Presence

- Be Prepared (8)
- Be Your Hero (6)
- Broken Bridge (1)
- Centering (4)
- Corner Speak (2)
- Down Cold (8)
- Embodied Aspiration (2)
- Fan Arms (2)
- Hand Rest (2)
- Head Hinge (1)
- Head Hinge with Voice (1)
- Hear Yourself (2)
- Launch (4)
- Keep the Conversation Going (8)
- Key Message (7)
- Key-Message You (9)
- Practice Rehearsal for Effective Q&A with Active Listening (8)
- Reverse Turtle Neck (1)
- Speak the Speech for Virtual Communication (10)
- Standing O (1)
- Stressful or Soothing (2)
- Style Selection (8)
- Subtle Subtext (2)
- Three-Act Play (9)

- Tune In (2)
- Virtual or Real: Key-Message a Meeting (10)
- Write; Don't Send (10)
- Your Inner Animal (5)

Feedback Loop— Thought-Emotion-Body

- Be Your Hero (6)
- Beach Walk (4)
- Belly Feel (3)
- Belly Imagine (3)
- Body Scan (2)
- Broken Bridge (1)
- Embodied Aspiration (2)
- Embodied Ick (2)
- Finish the Fantasy (9)
- Inner Ear (1)
- Habit Breaker (1)
- Head Hinge (1)
- The List of You (2)
- The List of Your Nemesis (2)
- Office Walk (4)
- Open Heart (2)
- Standing O (1)
- Stressful or Soothing (2)
- Take a Thought for a Dance (4)
- Take a Thought for a Walk (1)
- What If . . . ? (6)
- What if I . . . ?, Continued (9)
- Word Move (1)

Feet

- Beach Walk (4)
- Centering (4)
- Feeling Feet (4)
- Just an Inch! (1)

- Launch (4)
- Long Step/Short Step (4)
- Office Walk (4)
- Walk Copy (4)

Focus

- Belly Breath (2)
- Body Scan (2)
- Elephant Ears (1)
- The Flow: A Toe in the Stream (6)
- The Flow: Body *Now* (6)
- The Flow: Mind *Now* (6)
- Focus On (5)
- Inner Ear (1)
- Keep the Conversation Going (8)
- Take It All In (5)
- 10-Second Breath (2)
- Tune In (2)
- Tuning In to the Tuned Out (3)

Habits

- Body Scan (2)
- Broken Bridge (1)
- Focus On (5)
- Habit Breaker (1)
- Head Hinge (1)
- Just an Inch! (1)
- Long Step/Short Step (4)
- Office Walk (4)

Hands

- Get the Peanut Butter Off (2)
- Hand Rest (2)

Head

- Head Hinge (1)
- Head Hinge with Voice (1)
- Weighted Neck Stretch (2)

Heart
- Open Heart (2)
- Three-Act Play (9)

Hips
- Beach Walk (4)
- Belly Dance (4)
- Get the Peanut Butter Off (2)
- Open Hips (4)
- Seated Pelvic Tilt (4)
- Sitting Tall (4)
- Walk Copy (4)

Imagination
- Be Your Hero (6)
- Beach Walk (4)
- Belly Feel (3)
- Belly Imagine (3)
- Embodied Aspiration (2)
- Failure's Offspring (6)
- Finish the Fantasy (9)
- Go for a Walk (9)
- Open Heart (2)
- Safe-Place Sense Memory (5)
- The Seed of Failure (6)
- Take a Thought for a Dance (4)
- Take a Thought for a Walk (1)
- Walk Copy (4)
- What Did Failure Grow? (6)
- What If . . . ? (6)
- Word Move (1)
- Write Your Hero a Letter (6)
- Your Inner Animal (5)

Improvisation
- Center Control Towers (5)
- The Flow: Mind *Now* (6)
- Walk Copy (4)
- Word Move (1)

Jaw Tension
- Belly Breath (2)
- Head Hinge (1)
- Head Hinge with Voice
- Sweet Apricot: Jaw Relax (1)

Key Messaging
- Key Message Template (7)
- Metaphor/Simile Practice (7)
- Purpose and Audience (7)
- Virtual or Real: Key-Message a Meeting (10)
- What's the Title? (7)

Legs
- Beach Walk (4)
- Centering (4)
- Get the Peanut Butter Off (2)
- Just an Inch! (1)
- Launch (4)
- Long Step/Short Step (4)
- Office Walk (4)
- Walk Copy (4)

Listening
- Elephant Ears (1)
- Inner Ear (1)
- Keep the Conversation Going (8)
- Open Heart (2)
- Stressful or Soothing (2)
- Tune In (2)

Managing People
- Body Scan (2)
- Embodied Aspiration (2)
- Keep the Conversation Going (8)
- Key Message (7)
- Lions, Tigers, Bears, . . . and Puppies (5)

- Observation-Impact-Suggestion (8)
- Open Heart (2)
- Right Words (2)
- Soft Belly (3)
- Stressful or Soothing (2)
- Subtle Subtext (2)
- Virtual or Real: Key-Message
  a Meeting (10)
- Which Dominates, Being Liked
  or Respected? (9)
- Write; Don't Send (10)

Metaphors
- Metaphor/Simile Practice (7)

Muscle Memory
- Broken Bridge (1)
- Focus On (5)
- Head Hinge (1)
- Just an Inch! (1)
- Long Step/Short Step (4)
- Office Walk (4)

Navigating New Media
- Virtual or Real: Key-Message
  a Meeting (10)
- Write; Don't Send (10)

Negotiation Practices
- Keep the Conversation Going (8)
- Lions, Tigers, Bears, . . . and
  Puppies (5)

Networks
- The Web of You (9)
- Web Six Degrees of Separation (9)

Play
- Be an Elephant (Epilogue)

- Be Your Hero (6)
- Beach Walk (4)
- Belly Feel (3)
- Center Control Towers (5)
- Embodied Aspiration (2)
- Get the Peanut Butter Off (2)
- Go for a Walk (9)
- Ministry of Silly Walks (4)
- Take a Thought for a Dance (4)
- Walk Copy (4)
- What If . . . ? (6)
- Word Move (1)
- Your Inner Animal (5)

Point of View
- Be Your Hero (6)
- Beach Walk (4)
- Embodied Aspiration (2)
- Judge's Journal (1)
- Judge's Journal Replies (1)
- Office Walk (4)
- Take a Thought for a Walk (1)
- What Did Failure Grow? (6)
- What If . . . ? (6)

Posture
- Body Scan (2)
- The Butterfly (2)
- Centering (4)
- Embodied Aspiration (2)
- Fan Arms (2)
- Launch (4)
- Reverse Turtle Neck (1)
- Seated Pelvic Tilt (4)
- Sitting Tall (4)
- Weighted Neck Stretch (2)

Preparation for Public Speaking

- Be Prepared (8)
- Belly Breath (2)
- Breath with Arm Thrust (2)
- Down Cold (8)
- Embodied Aspiration (2)
- Get the Peanut Butter Off (2)
- Practice Rehearsal for Effective Q&A with Active Listening (8)
- Purpose and Audience (7)
- Speak the Speech for Virtual Communication (10)
- Standing O (1)
- Style Selection (8)
- 10-Second Breath (2)
- Torso Vibrate (2)

Problem Solving

- Detail the Key Messages (7)
- Finish the Fantasy (9)
- Judge's Journal Replies (1)
- Key Message (7)
- Key-Message You (9)
- Metaphor/Simile Practice (7)
- Virtual or Real: Key-Message a Meeting (10)
- The Web of You (9)
- What If . . . ? (6)
- Write; Don't Send (10)
- Write Your Hero a Letter (6)

Rehearsal Techniques

- Down Cold (8)
- Get the Peanut Butter Off (2)
- Hand Dance (2)
- Hand Watch (2)
- Lazy Lips Workout (2)

- Observation-Impact-Suggestion (8)
- Practice Rehearsal for Effective Q&A with Active Listening (8)
- Speak the Speech for Virtual Communication (10)
- Standing O (1)
- Torso Vibrate (2)

Relaxation

- Abdomen Vibrate (2)
- Bag of Sand (2)
- Be an Elephant (Epilogue)
- Beach Walk (4)
- Belly Breath (2)
- Body Scan (2)
- Chest Vibrate (2)
- Elephant Ears (1)
- Get the Peanut Butter Off (2)
- Safe-Place Sense Memory (5)
- Soft Belly (3)
- Standing O (1)
- Sweet Apricot: Jaw Relax (1)
- 10-Second Breath (2)
- Torso Vibrate (2)
- Tuning In to the Tuned Out (3)
- Weighted Neck Stretch (2)
- Wet Dog (1)

Releasing Blocks

Emotional

- Belly Feel (3)
- Embodied Aspiration (2)
- Finish the Fantasy (9)
- Judge's Journal Replies (1)
- The List of You (2)
- The List of Your Nemesis (2)
- Open Heart (2)
- Word Move (1)

Physical
- Abdomen Vibrate (2)
- Bag of Sand (2)
- Be an Elephant (Epilogue)
- Beach Walk (4)
- Belly Breath (2)
- Belly Dance (4)
- Body Scan (2)
- Chest Vibrate (2)
- Get the Peanut Butter Off (2)
- Open Heart (2)
- Open Hips (4)
- Soft Belly (3)
- Torso Vibrate (2)
- Tuning In to the Tuned Out (3)
- Word Move (1)

Self-Coaching/Self-Talk
- Embodied Aspiration (2)
- Failure's Offspring (6)
- Finish the Fantasy (9)
- Inner Ear (1)
- Judge's Journal (1)
- Judge's Journal Replies (1)
- Key-Message You (9)
- The List of You (2)
- The List of Your Nemesis (2)
- Out Loud (1)
- Right Words (2)
- The Seed of Failure (6)
- Take a Thought for a Walk (1)
- What Did Failure Grow? (6)

Self-Reflection/Self-Awareness
- Beach Walk (4)
- Belly Feel (3)
- Belly Imagine (3)
- Body Scan (2)

- Center Control Towers (5)
- Embodied Aspiration (2)
- Embodied Ick (2)
- Failure's Offspring (6)
- Finish the Fantasy (9)
- The Flow: A Toe in the Stream (6)
- The Flow: Mind *Now* (6)
- Focus On (5)
- Go for a Walk (9)
- Hear Yourself (2)
- Inner Ear (1)
- Judge's Journal (1)
- Judge's Journal Replies (1)
- Key-Message You (9)
- The List of You (2)
- The List of Your Nemesis (2)
- Mirror Talk (1)
- Office Walk (4)
- Open Heart (2)
- Out Loud (1)
- Right Words (2)
- Safe-Place Sense Memory (5)
- The Seed of Failure (6)
- Soft Belly (3)
- Stressful or Soothing (2)
- Take a Thought for a Walk (1)
- Tuning In to the Tuned Out (3)
- The Web of You (9)
- What Did Failure Grow? (6)
- What Does the Body Think? (9)
- What If . . . ? (6)
- What if I . . . ?, Continued (9)
- Which Dominates, Being Liked or Respected? (9)
- Word Move (1)
- Write Your Hero a Letter (6)
- Your Inner Animal (5)

Shoulders

- Center Control Towers (5)
- Fan Arms (2)
- Happy Shoulders/Sad Hips (5)

Speaking Up

- Breath with Arm Thrust (2)
- Embodied Aspiration (2)
- Out Loud (1)
- Sitting Tall (4)

Stage Fright—Managing, Conquering (also see Stress Reduction)

- Be Your Hero (6)
- Belly Breath (2)
- Embodied Aspiration (2)
- Focus On While Presenting (5)
- Get the Peanut Butter Off (2)
- Standing O (1)
- Take a Thought for a Dance (4)
- Take It All In (5)
- 10-Second Breath (2)

Strategic Thinking

- Key Message (7)
- Right Words (2)
- Style Selection (8)
- What If . . . ? (6)
- Write Your Hero a Letter (6)

Stress Reduction

- Abdomen Vibrate (2)
- Bag of Sand (2)
- Beach Walk (4)
- Belly Breath (2)
- Body Scan (2)
- Breath with Arm Thrust (2)
- Chest Vibrate (2)

- Elephant Ears (1)
- Embodied Aspiration (2)
- Get the Peanut Butter Off (2)
- Go for a Walk (9)
- Ministry of Silly Walks (4)
- Open Heart (2)
- Safe-Place Sense Memory (5)
- Soft Belly (3)
- Standing O (1)
- Take a Thought for a Dance (4)
- Take a Thought for a Walk (1)
- 10-Second Breath (2)
- Torso Vibrate (2)
- Tuning In to the Tuned Out (3)
- Weighted Neck Stretch (2)

Subtext

- Subtle Subtext (2)
- Subtle Text (2)
- Tone Talk (2)
- Tune In (2)

Telephone Conference Skills

- Corner Speak (2)
- Keep the Conversation Going (8)
- Key Message (7)
- Lazy Lips Workout (2)
- Purpose and Audience (7)
- Subtle Subtext (2)
- Tone Talk (2)
- Torso Vibrate (2)
- Virtual or Real: Key-Message a Meeting (10)

Tension Blocks Release

All Body

- Bag of Sand (2)
- Beach Walk (4)

- Belly Breath (2)
- Focus On (5)
- Tuning In to the Tuned Out (3)

Head
- Happy/Sad Mouth (1)
- Head Hinge (1)
- Sweet Apricot: Jaw Relax (1)

Neck
- Head Hinge (1)
- Head Hinge with Voice (1)
- Reverse Turtle Neck (1)
- Weighted Neck Stretch (2)

Shoulders
- Fan Arms (2)

Chest
- Open Heart (2)

Arms
- Get the Peanut Butter Off (2)

Hands
- Get the Peanut Butter Off (2)
- Hand Rest (2)

Torso
- Abdomen Vibrate (2)
- Belly Breath (2)
- Belly Dance (4)
- Broken Bridge (1)
- Get the Peanut Butter Off (2)
- Open Hips (4)
- Seated Pelvic Tilt (4)
- Soft Belly (3)
- 10-Second Breath (2)
- Torso Vibrate (2)
- Wet Dog (1)

Legs
- Get the Peanut Butter Off (2)
- Take a Thought for a Dance (4)

Feet
- Feeling Feet (4)

Tone
- Be Your Hero (6)
- Hear Yourself (2)
- Right Words (2)
- Stressful or Soothing (2)
- Tone Talk (2)
- Tune In (2)

Vocabulary
- Be Your Hero (6)
- Filler Be Gone! (2)
- Keep the Conversation Going (8)
- Key Message (7)
- Metaphor/Simile Practice (7)
- Right Words (2)
- Style Selection (8)
- Subtle Subtext (2)
- Subtle Text (2)
- Virtual or Real: Key-Message a Meeting (10)
- What's the Title? (7)

Vocal Mastery—Volume, Resonance, Tone, Enunciation
- Abdomen Vibrate (2)
- Belly Breath (2)
- Breath with Arm Thrust (2)
- Broken Bridge (1)
- Chest Vibrate (2)
- Corner Speak (2)
- Filler Be Gone! (2)
- Head Hinge with Voice (1)
- Hear Yourself (2)
- Lazy Lips Workout (2)
- Reverse Turtle Neck (1)

- Speak the Speech for Virtual Communication (10)
- Stressful or Soothing (2)
- Subtle Subtext (2)
- Sweet Apricot: Jaw Relax (1)

- Tone Talk (2)
- Torso Vibrate (2)
- Tune In (2)
- Wet Dog (1)
- Wet Dog Talking (2)

APPENDIX C
Selected Reading:
Books on the Voice

Berry, Cicely, *Voice and the Actor*, New York: Wiley, 1973.

Boston, Jane, and Rena Cook, *Breath in Action: The Art of Breath in Vocal and Holistic Practice*, London: Jessica Kingsley Publishers, 2009.

DeVore, Kate, and Starr Cookman, *The Voice Book: Caring for, Protecting, and Improving Your Voice*, Chicago: Chicago Review Press, 2009.

Lessac, Arthur, *The Use and Training of the Human Voice: A Bio-Dynamic Approach to Vocal Life*, 3rd ed., Mayfield Publishing Company, 1997.

Linklater, Kristin, *Freeing the Natural Voice*, Drama Book Publishers, 1976.

McClosky, David Blair, *Your Voice at Its Best: Enhancement of the Healthy Voice, Help for the Troubled Voice*, Waveland Press, 2011.

APPENDIX D
Additional
Worksheets

Exercise Name	Frequency Goal / Actual	Observations	Next Steps
	/		
	/		
	/		
	/		
	/		
	/		

Exercise Name	Frequency Goal / Actual	Observations	Next Steps
	/		
	/		
	/		
	/		
	/		
	/		

239

Exercise Name	Frequency Goal / Actual	Observations	Next Steps
	/		
	/		
	/		
	/		
	/		
	/		

Exercise Name	Frequency Goal / Actual	Observations	Next Steps
	/		
	/		
	/		
	/		
	/		
	/		

Exercise Name	Frequency Goal / Actual	Observations	Next Steps
	/		
	/		
	/		
	/		
	/		
	/		

Exercise Name	Frequency Goal / Actual	Observations	Next Steps
	/		
	/		
	/		
	/		
	/		
	/		

Exercise Name	Frequency Goal / Actual	Observations	Next Steps
	/		
	/		
	/		
	/		
	/		
	/		

244

Index

About the Author

Gina Barnett founded Barnett International, Inc., an executive communications consulting firm, after decades working in the professional theater. Coaching thought leaders in science, healthcare, finance, the arts, and technology, she consults around the globe with such organizations as Novartis, GSK, HSBC, the Guggenheim Foundation, the mainstage TED Conference, and the TED Fellows and Institute. Working with individuals from over 30 countries and cultures (Bangladesh, Japan, Brazil, Jordan, China, India, Argentina, Russia, and Thailand to name a few), bringing knowledge of the profound effects of presentational style and presence on oneself and on others. Her travels have only deepened her belief that communication excellence in today's global economy is essential for success and that leadership presence is a craft not a mystery that can be mastered.

She works, writes, plays—as well as *writes plays*—in New York City, where she and her husband live.